STATE RIGHTS IN
THE CONFEDERACY

THE UNIVERSITY OF CHICAGO PRESS
CHICAGO, ILLINOIS

—

THE BAKER & TAYLOR COMPANY
NEW YORK

THE CAMBRIDGE UNIVERSITY PRESS
LONDON

THE MARUZEN-KABUSHIKI-KAISHA
TOKYO, OSAKA, KYOTO, FUKUOKA, SENDAI

THE COMMERCIAL PRESS, LIMITED
SHANGHAI

STATE RIGHTS IN
THE CONFEDERACY

By

FRANK LAWRENCE OWSLEY, Ph.D.

Professor of History, Vanderbilt University

THE UNIVERSITY OF CHICAGO PRESS
CHICAGO ، ILLINOIS

COMPOSED AND PRINTED BY THE UNIVERSITY OF CHICAGO PRESS
CHICAGO, ILLINOIS, U.S.A.

TO MY WIFE
HARRIET CHAPPELL OWSLEY
WITHOUT WHOSE HELP THIS WORK
WOULD NOT HAVE BEEN POSSIBLE

PREFACE

For sixty years the student and casual reader of Civil War history have labored under the impression that the South was "overpowered by superior numbers." This volume attempts to present a different point of view, namely that the Confederacy failed from internal, political causes, mainly state rights. Having lectured on this theme before southern audiences, I know that this new aspect of the question, as I present it, is sometimes misunderstood as being an unfriendly attack upon the people who fought for the idea of state rights. To those who are inclined to feel that I am making such an attack, I wish to say that, by way of explanation, this is largely because I do not dwell upon the heroism and unselfishness in the Confederacy which has been the theme of countless volumes and is, therefore, common knowledge. I assume that knowledge and hasten on to take up certain political phases which may well be called "the seamy side" of Confederate history.

The chief sources from which the material for this book was drawn were the official records of

PREFACE

the Union and Confederate armies, *Journal of the Confederate Congress*, *Confederate Records of Georgia*, *History of the Several Regiments and Battalions of North Carolina in the Great War*, *Appleton's Cyclopaedia*, *Moore's Rebellion Record*, representative contemporary newspapers, such as: *Montgomery Weekly Advertiser*, *Montgomery Mail*, *Montgomery Confederation*, *Mobile Register*, *Richmond Whig*, *Richmond Examiner*, *Richmond Enquirer*, *Raleigh Standard*, *Charleston Mercury*, etc., contemporary diaries, especially Jones, Mrs. Chestnut, Mrs. Pryor, Russell, and H. V. Johnson, and the correspondence, speeches, and letters of the leaders.

I wish to express my gratitude to the Tennessee State Library, Vanderbilt University Library, University of Chicago Library, and the *Montgomery Advertiser* for the use of their various collections of material.

I wish also to acknowledge my indebtedness to Messrs. William E. Dodd, of the University of Chicago, and Walter L. Fleming, of Vanderbilt University, for reading the manuscript and offering valuable criticisms and advice.

Frank L. Owsley

Vanderbilt University
Nashville, Tennessee
May, 1925

viii

PREFACE TO SECOND IMPRESSION

Nearly six years have elapsed since the publication and ten since the writing of *State Rights in the Confederacy*. The book was widely reviewed. It stirred up controversy and in some quarters was hotly challenged.

Since the writing of the book, I have continued my researches in the field of Confederate history, and nothing that I have found weakens the fundamental conclusions reached a decade ago.

Perhaps the most convincing evidence I could offer—though not intended as such—that the Confederacy failed from internal causes is the larger companion volume, *King Cotton Diplomacy*, being brought out with the second impression of *State Rights*. *King Cotton Diplomacy*, I believe, will entirely explode the idea that the South was strangled by an effective blockade, for it challenges with supporting evidence the effectiveness of the Federal blockade.

There is, in fact, only one change I should

like to make were I to re-write the book: I
should like to emphasize the irritability of President Davis, due to frail health, as a factor in
plunging him into quarrels with men like Brown
and Vance.

FRANK LAWRENCE OWSLEY

February 26, 1931

TABLE OF CONTENTS

INTRODUCTION

There is an old saying that the seeds of death are sown at our birth. This was true of the southern Confederacy, and the seeds of death were state rights. The principle on which the South based its actions before 1861 and on which it hoped to base its future government was its chief weakness. If a monument is ever erected as a symbolical gravestone over the "lost cause" it should have engraved upon it these words: "Died of State Rights." We are in the habit of ascribing as the causes of the failure of the Confederacy the blockade, lack of industrial development and resources, breakdown of transportation, inadequate financial system, and so on, all of which are fundamental; yet, in spite of all of these, if the political system of the South had not broken down under the weight of an impracticable doctrine put into practice in the midst of a revolution, the South might have established its independence. If the leaders had been able to bury their differences as to the theory of government, if they had allowed the Confederate government the same freedom as that of the Federal (harassed though the Federal government was by internal strife) during the space of the war, it would have been almost an impossibility for the South to suffer defeat. But the Stephenses, Toombs, Browns, and Vances could not wait till after the war to try out their theories and air their differences; they had not "the ability to keep the ultimate aim in view even in adversity, and to see over and beyond the present calamity into the far-distant future." As the homely old saying puts it, "They could not see the forest for the trees." Insisting thus upon the theoretical rights of their states, they sowed dissension among the people and destroyed all spirit of co-operation, finally, between the states and the Confederate government, and, at times, arrayed local against central government as if each had been an unfriendly foreign power.

In using the term "state rights," both state sovereignty and state rights as used in the days of Jefferson and Calhoun are included, for the leaders were seldom consistent in their claims:

one time they would act upon the Calhoun theory of the absolute sovereignty of a state, while at another time the same men merely insisted upon the rigid division of powers between the state and central governments in accordance with the Jeffersonian doctrine—insisted with the tenacity and spirit of Shylock. But whether they acted upon the state-rights or state-sovereignty theory the practical results were the same: the state assumed or tried to assume functions whose exercise must of necessity devolve upon the central government, in any successful war against a strong antagonist; and the Confederacy was paralyzed, and, as we have already seen, the whole people were demoralized and embittered against each other and their governments by the controversies involved.

This assumption by the states of the power of the central government and the controversies that ensued extended to practically every field of activity connected in any way with the conduct of the war. Instead of pooling its resources of men and equipment in the hands of the Confederate government, each state insisted upon the right to maintain "troops of war" and, at times, with-

3

drew thousands of men and sorely needed arms from the general service and employed them for local defense, thereby weakening the Confederate government without gaining the equivalent (for, in most instances, these state troops were worthless). Not only did the states insist upon maintaining their own troops, they also insisted upon certain rights over their troops in Confederate service, such as the appointment of officers, the supplying of clothing and equipment, which resulted in unequal distribution. The state-rights leaders put all sorts of impediments in the way of Confederate impressment of supplies, and finally contributed largely to the complete breakdown of the impressment system. They prevented the execution, ofttimes, of the conscription laws and the laws suspending the writ of habeas corpus. There were controversies over other matters, but these mentioned above were the most fundamental, and it will be the purpose of the following chapters to follow out in detail the struggles that raged about these questions and the results of the struggles.

CHAPTER I
LOCAL DEFENSE

The military frontiers of the Confederacy stretched over many thousands of miles. Every state save Tennessee and Arkansas had long reaches of undefended seacoast, Florida alone having practically as much as the Union. Then there was the upper tier of Confederate states whose borders lay alongside the hostile frontiers of the Union, penetrated by navigable rivers radiating into the heart of the country. As if this were not enough exposure for the newborn republic, Texas and Arkansas were frontier states; to the north of them, in the territories of New Mexico, Arizona, and Indian Territory, lived many wild tribes of the aborigines, while to the west of Texas lived the half-breed Mexicans, whose depredations under the leadership of the chieftain, Cortinas,[1] were keeping the Rio

[1] *Montgomery Weekly Advertiser*, March 30, 1861; *The War of the Rebellion* (a compilation of the Official Records of the Union and Confederate armies Washington, 1880–1901), Ser. 4, Vol. I, p. 74. To be cited henceforth as O. R.

Grande country in constant turmoil. Last, but, to the southern people apprehensive of servile insurrection, not least in importance, was the "home front," liable at any moment to become the most horrible and bloody battle-ground of the war. If one can visualize this situation and keep in mind the fact that the people were thoroughly steeped in the doctrines of state rights and local patriotism, he will be prepared for the inevitable military policy that undertook the defense of all these far-flung lines. The "sovereign states" built up small armies of their own, inefficient and undisciplined, withdrawing at times a hundred thousand or more men, together with arms and equipment to fit them out, all of which were sorely needed on the battle front.

However, the Confederate government did not accept this individualistic policy with meekness. Its leaders, being in a position to see the whole situation, made a stupendous effort to gather in their hands the reins of power necessary for success and to obtain possession of the men and material retained in the state forces. The constant pull of the states to retain as large forces as possible and the counterpull of the Confederate government, with the general-staff point of view, to force the states to disgorge resulted in a veritable tug of war between the central and local governments.[1]

The study of the problem of local defense falls naturally into two periods: (1) from secession to the passage of the first conscript law in 1862, and (2) from the adoption of the conscript law until the war ended.

1. JANUARY, 1861, TO APRIL, 1862

The period that ends with the first conscript law may be characterized by two distinct phases: (a) the withholding by the states from Confederate service of arms and munitions of war, and (b) the withholding of men.

a) ARMS

There were on hand two available supplies of arms and munitions of war in the South when the Confederacy was organized, and both of these were held by the states. There were the

[1] See *Century Magazine*, November, 1896, and February, 1897, for opinions of Duncan Rose, General Stephen D. Lee, Brigadier General E. P. Alexander, Major General O. O. Howard, and General Buell, as to the effects of "dispersion" caused by local defense.

arms taken with the United States forts and arsenals, which were distributed among the states about as follows: 47,327 in Louisiana, 19,455 in Alabama, 22,469 in South Carolina, 22,714 in Georgia, 10,000 in Arkansas, 37,000 in North Carolina,[1] and 35,000 in Texas.[2] There were also a few thousand in Virginia and scattered around in other states, making a total of about 190,000 small arms, many of which were old-fashioned and of little use until repaired.[3] In addition to the arms thus captured, each state had on hand a supply, part of which had been purchased immediately after John Brown's raid and the election of Lincoln. Alabama had, during the winter of 1861, purchased 9,000 stand of arms, 10 brass cannon, 2 columbiads, and a large quantity of ammunition,[4] which, added to the

[1] O. R., Ser. 4, Vol. I, p. 292; see Walter Clark (ed.), *Histories of the Several Regiments and Battalions from N.C. in the Great War 1861–65* (Raleigh, 1901), I, 40–43, for North Carolina (cited henceforth as *N.C. Regiments*).

[2] *Confederation* (Montgomery), June 21, 1861.

[3] For instance, there were 20,000 rifles at Harper's Ferry with the stocks destroyed. J. B. Jones, *A Rebel War Clerk's Diary at the Confederate Capital* (Philadelphia, 1866), I, ·78 (cited henceforth as Jones, *Diary*), gives the total number of arms as only 150,000, but this is plainly a rough guess.

[4] O. R., Ser. 4, Vol. I, p. 52.

arms already on hand, made no bad show. Mississippi, already equipped with 2,127 rifles and other small arms, purchased about this time 5,000 stand of muskets.[1] Texas had several thousand in addition to a large supply of private arms.[2] Georgia[3] and North Carolina[4] each apparently had several thousand, and South Carolina had 11,000, just purchased,[5] and had an old stock that was in the hands of the militia.[6] Virginia had on hand 100,000 stand of small arms in the fall of 1860 and evidently made extensive purchases afterward.[7] In addition to these available supplies there were a large number of private arms in the South, due to the rural and frontier character of the section. But at best the supply of munitions of war was definitely limited. Yet if the individual states had immediately placed the arms in their possession in

[1] O. R., Ser. 4, Vol. I, pp. 63, 67, 68.

[2] Ibid., pp. 713–22.

[3] Ibid., pp. 319, 332, 350, 355, 366, 367, 401, 402, 473, 491, 1046, 1047, 1063–67.

[4] North Carolina Regiments, I, 40–43.

[5] O. R., Ser. 4, Vol. I, p. 479.

[6] Ibid., pp. 634–36; Ibid., Ser. 1, Vol. I, p. 265.

[7] Ibid., Ser. 4, Vol. I, pp. 379–93.

9

the hands of the Confederate armies, if the state authorities had made the proper effort to obtain the private arms of the citizen instead of discouraging him from selling them to Confederate agents, the Confederate government would have been able to put a much larger army in the field in 1861.

Theoretically, the states did transfer the arms and munitions captured with the United States arsenals, but in actual practice the several governors each disposed of a large part of these arms according to the interests of his own state or according to his own judgment.[1]

As to the arms actually owned by the states, the governors either refused to allow them to be carried out of the state, or gave them up reluctantly and sparingly. In March, 1861, Governor A. B. Moore of Alabama wrote Secretary Walker, who had applied to the Governor for arms, that he was not prepared to say what the state convention then in session would do about the matter, but that he was "inclined to the opinion that they should be retained by the state to enable her to meet any emergency and protect

[1] *Montgomery Mail*, May 14, 1861; O. R., Ser. 4, Vol. I, pp. 228, 292.

and defend her citizens."[1] Again on July 4, 1861, the Governor found it out of the question to arm 3,000 men called out by the Confederate government for general service, because, as he said, "it leaves the state almost defenseless";[2] but at the same time he was able to arm six regiments and 2,500 other special emergency troops for a defense of the coast which was in no immediate danger.[3]

Governor Thomas Moore, of Louisiana, informed Secretary Walker on May 20, 1861, after the latter had besought the Governor to arm a few thousand Confederate troops being raised in that state, that he was doubtful whether he would arm any more troops for general service, as he was "emphatically unwilling to leave the state without sufficient arms for home protection." At this moment the Governor had, apparently, a supply of arms lying idle in the state arsenal.[4] Again in July he refused to arm five or six regiments for the Confederacy because, he said, it would take all the guns in the arsenal, "and surely we ought not to be without arms

---

[1] O. R., Ser. 4, Vol. I, p. 121.   [3] Ibid., pp. 702, 704–5.
[2] Ibid., p. 420.   [4] Ibid., p. 337.

when we may expect an invasion ourselves in the fall."[1]

Nor was Mississippi any more generous than the other states in giving up her arms and munitions of war to the central government. On July 17, Governor Pettus wired Secretary Walker, who as usual was out in his futile quest for state help, that he had no power under the state law to arm the regiments just raised at Iuka.[2] The persistent refusal of his own state to supply Confederate troops with arms, or, in rare cases where it did supply them, its continuous discrimination in favor of short-term organizations, at length evoked a rebuke from President Davis.[3] Governor Pettus' reply was that he had only been carrying out the state law and the orders of the military board which laid the injunction upon the Governor that "no arms should be given to any companies until all the companies mustered into the service of the state were armed." Only in very rare cases, he added, had the military board allowed a departure from these orders.[4]

North Carolina, like the other seaboard

[1] O. R., Ser. 4, Vol. I, p. 422.   [2] Ibid., p. 484.
[3] Ibid., p. 712.   [4] Ibid., pp. 712–13.

states, lived in constant dread of a mammoth expedition against her coast, and she soon began to discourage the removal of her arms into the other states. In the spring of 1862 the Governor became so much concerned over the matter that he issued a belligerent proclamation against the purchase of arms or the impressment of any kind of military equipment by Confederate agents. He promised to use force, if it became necessary, to protect the citizens against the Confederate government.[1] Not only was he unwilling for them to leave the state, but in January, 1862, he was compelled, he said, "in view of the immediate and pressing necessity for arms for our defense" to ask the return of a quantity of arms that had been taken out of the state into Virginia.[2]

Governor Pickens of South Carolina wrote to Secretary of War Benjamin in September, 1861, that he felt that the state was not able to arm any more Confederate troops because it had to arm the 15,000 state troops.[3] Not satisfied with

[1] *Appleton's Annual Cyclopaedia* (1862), p. 660 (cited henceforth as *Annual Cyclopaedia*).

[2] O. R., Ser. 4, Vol. I, pp. 827–28.

[3] *Ibid.*, pp. 624, 634, 635; see also *ibid.*, p. 479.

keeping 15,000 stand of arms out of general service, he requested the actual return of some that had been taken out of the state.[1]

Tennessee, in the first few months, not only contributed no arms to the Confederate government, but actually received 6,000 stand with which to equip her state organizations who steadily refused to be mustered into Confederate service.[2] Texas refused to comply with requisitions from the Confederate authorities,[3] and in Arkansas the same situation existed. General Hindman notified President Davis that "the state authorities refuse arms of any kind, retaining them for the militia."[4]

Virginia, with her 100,000 stand of small arms and the Harper's Ferry machinery, together with other quantities of war material, showed the same reluctance in pooling her military equipment. The state authorities refused for a while to issue any of the tools and lead stored in the armory at Richmond, and Major Gorgas, Confederate munition chief, complained that the refusal had done "great injury to the

[1] O. R., Ser. 1, Vol. VI, p. 372.   [3] Ibid., Ser. 1, Vol. III, p. 623.
[2] Ibid., Ser. 4, Vol. I, pp. 358, 479.   [4] Ibid., p. 588.

common defense";[1] and when he suggested that
the stock of small arms belonging to Virginia,
stored in the Richmond armory, be transferred
to the Confederate authorities for general issue,
Secretary of State Munford quickly rejected the
proposal. Virginia, he protested, "wishes to reserve the arms now left in the armory for a case
of emergency, when it may be necessary to give
them to her unarmed militia."[2] Finally, because
of haggling on the part of the Virginia authorities, the most priceless months of Confederate
history were allowed to slip by before the Harper's Ferry and Richmond armory machinery
was transferred to the central government.[3]

Georgia not only proposed to keep what she
needed of the supply of arms within the state
but also to get as much more as possible out
of the Confederate government. Furthermore,
Governor Brown, in carrying out this selfish
policy, did not refrain from engaging in frequent,
unnecessary, and far-fetched quarrels with the
sorely beset Richmond government. With no

[1] *Ibid.*, Ser. 4, Vol. I, pp. 469–73.

[2] *Ibid.*, p. 511; see also *ibid.*, p. 722.

[3] *Ibid.*, pp. 358, 468–73, 476, 481, 482, 488, 489, 491, 492, 504–12, 530, 534.

uncertain motives he promptly "sat upon" the attempt of volunteers who had not been organized through his office to carry state arms out of Georgia. In May, 1861, he issued a proclamation that any officer who permitted or encouraged his men to carry state arms out of Georgia would be punished to the limit of the law.[1] The Governor also put in a claim for 29,000 pounds of powder stored in the Confederate arsenal at Augusta,[2] for he was determined that the state should have what belonged to it if it broke up the whole system of defense worked out in Richmond. However, the Confederate authorities would not deliver the powder before making an inquiry as to the facts in the case,[3] since powder was a very important commodity at the time. Whereupon Brown, angered by the delay, ordered the state arsenal at Savannah closed to all Confederate officials. His injunction to the arsenal keeper was "not to issue anything to the order of a Confederate officer

[1] O. R., Ser. 1, Vol. LII, Part II, p. 97; see *ibid.*, Ser. 4, Vol. I, pp. 319, 332, 350, 355, 366, 367, 401, 402, 473, 491 for controversy with the Confederate authorities over this question, also below.

[2] *Ibid.*, Ser. 4, Vol. I, p. 368.

[3] *Ibid.*, pp. 406, 407, 410, 411.

for the present."[1] Secretary Walker protested against such an abrupt procedure. Brown's reply indicated that the arsenal at Savannah had been closed in retaliation for the delay of the Secretary in releasing the powder claimed by the state at Augusta. Besides, without reference to other issues, Brown reminded Walker that "the arsenal and its contents are the property of the state" and that no Confederate officer had any rights there except at the sufferance of state authorities. In plain English, the arsenal belonged to Georgia, and it was nobody's business outside of Georgia as to what it pleased her to do with it.[2]

In April, 1862, Brown wrote Secretary of War Randolph asking the return of all of the rifles in the hands of the twelve-months troops whose term was soon to expire. He was not willing, he said, that the superior model rifles belonging to Georgia should be thrown into the Confederate arsenals for general issue. Then he added, figuratively lowering his voice into a knowing whisper: "If I have not mistaken your character you belong to that class of statesmen

---

[1] *Ibid.*, p. 401.　　　[2] *Ibid.*, p. 416.

known as state-rights men. I cannot, therefore, doubt what will be your decision of this question."[1] Outside of the fact that the twelve-months troops would soon be returning to Georgia, there was another reason why Brown raised the issue at this particular time: the Confederate Congress had passed a law requiring that all arms of the twelve-months or other troops whose term expired before the termination of the war should be kept within control of the President.[2] This law Brown evidently expected to question when he wrote Randolph, and undoubtedly he looked to the new Secretary of War for substantial aid in defeating its terms. But Randolph proved an apostate, at least in the opinion of Joe Brown, for he assured the Governor that "the exigencies of the times require many things which would under other circumstances be wholly unjustifiable . . . .," and that the act retaining the state arms within control of the President was one of the things necessary. He also dropped a hint to the factious Brown that a little patience and forbearance would mend matters very greatly.[3]

[1] O. R., Ser. 4, Vol. I, pp. 1046–47.   [3] Ibid., pp. 1058–59.
[2] Ibid., p. 1059.

Not content with retaining her own arms and a good part of those captured with the United States arsenals, Georgia attempted to obtain possession of Confederate cargoes of rifles that landed in her ports. The hysteria caused by rumors of a gigantic expedition against Brunswick gripped the people in the summer and fall of 1861. Apparently, Governor Brown was largely responsible for this, because he was continuously advertising the exposed condition of Georgia's coast. He called wildly for help, dancing a frantic jig up and down Georgia and accusing the Confederate government of gross neglect. If he could not get the Confederate government to return the Georgia boys in Virginia to protect their sacred homes and "rally around the green graves of their sires," he demanded that it give him plenty of rifles to arm those still at home. On September 18, 1861, he wired Benjamin to supply him with arms sufficient to equip four regiments for local defense. He suggested that he be allowed to help himself from the Confederate cargo just landed at Savannah.[1] Benjamin promptly wired him

[1] *Ibid.*, p. 614.

19

that this cargo was wanted for the poorly armed
troops in Virginia where real fighting was being
done.[1] But Joe Brown, who was successfully attempting to bring under his control the entire
management of the coast defense of Georgia,[2]
could not let such a rare opportunity escape to
get something at the expense of the central
government: he apparently induced the Confederate General Lawton, by the application of
high pressure,[3] to seize the cargo and place the
rifles in the hands of the local-defense troops.[4]
Lawton immediately notified Adjutant General
Cooper that the pressing necessity in Georgia
had forced him to seize these arms. He pictured
the people to be in a state of the "greatest alarm
at the intelligence, which seems reliable, that the
mammoth expedition now being fitted out in
New York is intended for Brunswick, on the
lower part of the coast of Georgia." The cargo

[1] O. R., Ser. 4, Vol. I, p. 615.

[2] *Ibid.*, Ser. 1, Vol. VI, p. 307.

[3] O. R., Ser. 4, Vol. I, p. 668. Brown had shown Lawton a message
from Richmond that convinced the latter of an imminent invasion. From
the well-known tactics of Brown one can readily understand what that
persistent individual was up to.

[4] *Ibid.*, pp. 617–18.

was needed to arm the thousands of able-bodied men being called out by Brown.[1] Secretary of War Benjamin, though the hands were those of Esau, recognized the voice of Jacob. He peremptorily ordered Lawton to recover at once all but a thousand rifles, with the caustic remark, evidently intended for the officious Brown who had been tampering with the Confederate general, "that it is scarcely necessary to observe that if the government cannot have its property intended for public defense landed or deposited at any point of the Confederacy without being exposed to having it seized and appropriated to meet supposed local exigencies it would be better to abandon at once all attempts to conduct the defense of the country on an organized system and deliver over the control of the military to the local militia and popular meetings."[2] But Governor Brown, who only thrived upon such words as these, did all in his power to grab the next cargo that landed in Georgia.[3]

The results of such a policy were disastrous. With the enthusiasm of the year 1861 (almost

[1] *Ibid*.   [2] *Ibid*., pp. 624–25.

[3] *Ibid*., Ser. 1, Vol. VI, pp. 318–19..

without a parallel in history) the Confederate government could have placed an army of perhaps 600,000 men in the field within a few months if it had had the arms. The several reports of the Secretary of War bear out this rather bold assertion. Secretary Walker, in his report of July 24, 1861, said:

It is with mingled feelings of pleasure and regret that this Department mentions the fact that many more have come forward to volunteer for the war than it was possible for the government to arm. From the applications on file in this office there can be no doubt that if arms were only furnished no less than 200,000 additional volunteers for the war would be found in our ranks in less than two months.[1]

Secretary Benjamin, who succeeded Walker in the fall of 1861, stated in his report of December 14 that when he assumed control of the war department it was not unusual "to refuse offers of 5,000 men per day";[2] and in March, 1862, he expressed the opinion to President Davis that he could put 350,000 additional men in the field if arms could be had.[3] But the arms were not to

[1] O. R., Ser. 4, Vol. I, p. 497; cf. *ibid.*, p. 349.   [2] *Ibid.*, p. 795.

[3] *Ibid.*, p. 970; *ibid.*, p. 1168; *ibid.*, Ser. 1, Vol. VII, p. 807. A prominent author of the *History of North Carolina Regiments* says that at least 100,000 more men would have been in the ranks by 1862 if arms had been furnished. *North Carolina Regiment*, Vol. I, pp. 40-43.

be had, mainly because the states refused to part with them, and only about half of 600,000 went into the Confederate armies before 1862. The result was that Albert Sidney Johnston[1] in the West had to lie idle at Bowling Green when with a few more thousand, as he lamented, he would have been able to take the offensive, and "Tennessee, the valley of the Mississippi, and the Confederacy" would have been safe; and Joe Johnston and Beauregard in the East were unable to move for lack of men.[2] The initial advantages of better trained soldiery and better generals[3] were lost and the popular enthusiasm

[1] O. R., Ser. 1, Vol. VII, pp. 794-95.

[2] *Montgomery Weekly Advertiser*, August 31, 1861.

[3] The statement that the South had the better generals and the better-trained soldiery at the outbreak of the war will probably go unquestioned at the present day, for all recall the fact that the prominent southern families took a special pride in sending their sons to West Point and to the several well-equipped military academies in the South, and that the mass of southern people were accustomed to the use of the rifle and pistol, and to horse-back riding, and to other exercises closely related to military training, and moreover, the institution of slavery tended to develop the militant temperament. This condition would naturally lead one to expect the South to show the advantage at first, and the fact that Lincoln changed generals after almost every important battle until those splendid leaders, Thomas Sheridan, Sherman, and Grant were brought to the top showed that the Confederacy came up to expectations. The situation is well characterized by the following quotations from the *New*

for war was dissipated: state rights had reaped its first harvest.

b) MEN

But no sooner had the Confederacy begun to obtain arms in sufficient quantities to meet the exigencies of the situation than another obstacle placed in its path by state rights loomed up: the war department could not get men. The individual states had capitalized the enthusiasm and the fears of the people and had caught the overflow in their own local military organizations. These organizations had their inception at the very beginning of secession. They had been very small at first and had interfered little with the Confederate attempts to build up an army, except of course in the matter of arms, but gradually they grew in size and importance until they absorbed a great part of the man power that should have gone into the general service. An account of these organizations, state by state,

---

York Tribune: "Most of them (southerners) have been trained from the cradle to consider personal bravery the very first essential of manly character, and skill in the use of arms the first necessity of a gentleman. The revolver and rifle have been their plaything from boyhood. . . . . They have many of the very best of our late army officers and their soldiers will at first be better led and better handled than ours." (Quoted in the *Montgomery Weekly Advertiser,* May 14, 1861.)

will help us to an understanding of their importance as a factor in the overthrow of the Confederacy.

In January, 1861, Governor A. B. Moore suggested to the legislature that Alabama should have a "regular army" for its protection in case of trouble with the United States growing out of secession.[1] A few days after this the state convention adopted this suggestion of the Governor and authorized the organization of a state army.[2] As a result, Moore was able in the fall of that year to report that the local troops—not to be confused with the militia—consisted of six regiments, and 2,500 other special troops, all well-armed and equipped, and several other units in the process of formation.[3] About the same time that the Alabama convention authorized the formation of a regular army, Louisiana made a similar step,[4] with about the same results.[5] In

[1] O. R., Ser. 4, Vol. I, p. 50.

[2] *Ibid.*, Ser. 1, Vol. LII, Part II, p. 15.

[3] *Ibid.*, Vol. I, pp. 702, 704-5; cf. *Annual Cyclopaedia* (1862), p. 9, and Miller, *History of Alabama*, pp. 156, 157, 179, for references to state troops.

[4] O. R., Ser. 4, Vol. I, pp. 172-73, 177-78.

[5] *Ibid.*, pp. 753, 754, 755; *ibid.*, Ser. 1, Vol. LIII, p. 612.

Mississippi, by the first of March, 1861, there were, according to Governor Pettus' count, between thirty and forty companies of state troops;[1] and by the passage of the first conscription law this force had been built up to almost 5,000 regularly enlisted state troops.[2] North Carolina kept up a large force, under constant fear of an attack from the sea. In the late spring of 1862 the state forces numbered 10,000 men[3] in actual service and 10,000 organized, ready to be called out,[4] making a total of 20,000. During the first year of the war there were between 15,000 and 20,000 state troops in South Carolina,[5] in addition to the militia and Confederate troops in that state. Governor Harris of Tennessee reported on May 28, 1861, several thousand state troops, all of whom seemed unwilling to enter the general service;[6] and on July 31 the

[1] O. R., Ser. 4, Vol. I, p. 174; cf. *ibid.*, p. 63.

[2] *Ibid.*, Ser. 4, Vol. II, pp. 178–79.

[3] *Ibid.*, Vol. I, p. 1092; cf. *ibid.*, pp. 827–28.

[4] *North Carolina Regiments*, I, 8–12. Ten thousand were turned over at the time of conscription, but 6 infantry, 3 artillery, and 1 cavalry regiment were left in the state. *Ibid.*, p. 12.

[5] O. R., Ser. 1, Vol. I, pp. 624, 634–35; *Annual Cyclopaedia* (1862), p. 759.

[6] O. R., Ser. 1, Vol. I, p. 358.

Tennessee adjutant general's report showed 19,400 infantry, 2,079 cavalry, and 558 artillery in the state forces.[1] Virginia had, according to the paymaster of state troops, 40,000 men thus organized on about the first of July.[2] Arkansas had usually about 8,000 state troops during this period;[3] and it was due largely to the divided authority over state and Confederate forces that Missouri and most of Arkansas were lost to the South during the first year of the war.[4] Texas, as we might expect from her exposed frontiers, insisted upon keeping a well-organized state force.[5]

Georgia, in all probability, kept no more local troops than South Carolina, or even North Carolina; but Governor Brown, whose patriot-

[1] *Ibid.*, Ser. 1, Vol. LII, Part II, pp. 123–24.

[2] *Ibid.*, Ser. 4, Vol. I, pp. 860–63; cf. *ibid.*, pp. 963, 1114–15, and *ibid.*, Ser. 1, Vol. LI, Part II, p. 495. These troops were mustered into Confederate service, as sometimes happened in the other states, but they retained their local character, being mustered only for limited periods and for state defense. The object of being carried on the Confederate rolls was to obtain Confederate pay.

[3] *Ibid.*, Ser. 1, Vol. III, pp. 595, 732; Vol. VIII, p. 748; Vol. XIII, pp. 29–32.

[4] *Ibid.*, Vol. XIII, pp. 29–32.

[5] *Ibid.*, Ser. 4, Vol. I, pp. 250–52, 717, 978–79.

ism reached very little farther than the borders of his own political opportunities which coincided with the boundaries of the state of Georgia, assumed the attitude now, as always, of "every man for himself and the devil for us all." In the early part of 1861, the Georgia state convention under the guidance of the energetic Governor provided for a state force of two regiments of regulars and ten thousand volunteer troops to be held in readiness for any emergency that might threaten the safety and peace of the state.[1] Even at this early period, Brown showed himself alert for symptoms of encroachments upon Georgia's rights. The Confederate government had just taken over, by law, the defense of all the states; in short, had assumed its legitimate control of war, and the Governor was very careful to point out to the state convention that there were very definite limits upon the powers of the Confederate government in the matter of controlling and directing the defense of the state of Georgia. On March 15 he reminded the convention that it was one of Georgia's reserved rights to have a well-organized force, and that in joining the Con-

[1] O. R., Ser. 4, Vol. I, pp. 167-68.

federacy she had not surrendered the right to protect herself when she was threatened.[1] As the year wore on the fear of invasion grew, especially, as we have already seen, under the inspiration of Brown.[2] And as we will remember, he conceived the ambitious plan of directing the whole coastal defense himself. In carrying out this plan he demanded that the Confederate government move no more native troops from the state;[3] he demanded that Stovall's battalion be returned from Lynchburg, Virginia,[4] and he demanded other impossible and foolish things. In the meanwhile, he recruited an entire division and organized the coast defense without reference to Confederate plans.[5] General Lawton, of the Confederate service, wrote Secretary Benjamin that Brown was planning to put General W. H. T. Walker, who had left the Confederate service embittered against the government, in charge of the state defense, and he was so deject-

[1] O. R., Ser. 4, Vol. I, p. 168.

[2] See p. 19.

[3] O. R., Ser. 1, Vol. LI, Part II, p. 359.

[4] *Ibid.*, Vol. VI, p. 284.

[5] *Ibid.*, p. 307; *Confed. Records of Ga.*, II, 93–95, 131–32, 138–44, 146, 154.

ed over the prospect that he predicted disaster and asked to be relieved of his place.[1] There is no way of knowing the exact size of Brown's state army during this period, for it was composed of all kinds of troops, militia, short-term volunteers, and regularly enlisted men. However, in the spring of 1862, when the conscript law was passed which robbed the Governor of some of his troops, there were, according to Brown's report to Secretary Randolph, 8,000 regularly enlisted men in state service,[2] and many had already served out enlistments and gone home.

This policy of each state's maintaining its own troops for local defense, and its effect upon the general Confederate service was well summed up by Secretary of War Benjamin in one of his reports. Due to the great enthusiasm of the people, he said, the Confederate government was just on the eve of success in putting in the field a powerful army when it

was embarrassed and impeded by a very unexpected cause. In several of the states the governors, apprehensive of at-

[1] O. R., Ser. 1, Vol. VI, p. 284.
[2] *Ibid.*, Ser. 4, Vol. I, pp. 1063, 1067.

tack at home and actuated by the natural desire of aiding in the defense of their own states, failed to perceive that the only effective means of attaining that end was by a concentration of the common strength under one head, and that an attempt by each state to make a separate defense against so powerful an enemy . . . . could result in nothing but the defeat of each in detail. In disregard of so obvious a truth several of the states undertook to raise independent armies to repel invasion, retained at home arms and munitions, and called for volunteers for short terms . . . . for service within the state. The fatal effect of so short-sighted a policy became instantly apparent. Companies already organized and ready to be mustered into Confederate service for the war marched out of the camps of rendezvous to enlist in the state service for three, four, or six months.[1]

2. APRIL, 1862, TO APRIL, 1865

No sooner had the conscript law of April, 1862 broken up the state military organizations than several of the states began to rebuild them. Presently, as a result of this movement, there were as many men held back for local defense as there had been the first year of the war. Yet

[1] *Ibid.*, Vol. I, p. 795; cf. Brown's message to Georgia assembly, December 5, 1861, in *Confederate Records of Georgia*, II, 154. Louisiana, North Carolina, Virginia, Tennessee, and probably other states, he said "have called into the field large numbers of state troops to repel invasion and protect their property." This policy of local defense was evidently generally known throughout the Confederacy.

these formidable aggregations of state troops were absolutely worthless from all points of view: they were of no value to the Confederacy and they were of none to their state. General Brandon described them as "being composed of men who have been skulking from the service" by hiding in the local organizations under state protection; and who had no discipline, since they were amenable only "to their own courts-martial composed of the same class of men," whose decisions were always "in accord with the general feeling of the men and officers." The men, he said, were always "going and coming when they please," and they were "but little better than an armed mob." Not being subject to Confederate courts-martial, the generals could not enforce discipline and order, "and disaster and disgrace will result when they are brought into the field."[1]

Nine-tenths of the men in many of the organizations were subject to general service, which, added to the notorious inefficiency and cowardice of such organizations, made it absolutely necessary that the Confederate government should obtain control of them, both to

[1] O. R., Ser. 4, Vol. III, p. 740.

obtain men fit for recruiting its armies and for the purpose of discipline and unity of purpose. So the Richmond government set out to accomplish this end, and the whole period from the beginning of conscription till the end of the war is marked by its desperate but futile efforts to extend its control over state troops. Secretary of War Seddon sounded the keynote of this policy in a circular letter to the state governors. He said: "The numerically superior armies of the enemy confronting us in the field at all the most important points render essential for success in our great struggle . . . . greater concentration of our forces and their withdrawal in a measure from the purposes of local defense."[1] Let us follow out the successful efforts of each state, after the first conscript act, to rehabilitate its local troops, and the unsuccessful efforts of the Confederacy to obtain control of these troops.

In the summer of 1862 Alabama, under the direction of Governor Shorter, began to salvage its old military organizations and to rebuild them, at first out of material not taken into the

[1] *Ibid.*, Vol. II, p. 580.

Confederate service. On August 28 the Governor called for five hundred men to guard a certain vital point in the state where several public works were located.[1] In December the Governor followed up this call with a stirring proclamation for men and boys to volunteer for the defense of their state.[2] There was no intention, at first, of absorbing conscript material into the local units, but the desire for men was great, so that no embarrassing questions were usually asked when a man presented himself for local defense. One step led to another, until presently Governor Shorter came out with the bold request that the war department allow him to enlist for state defense all the conscripts in the counties of Barbour, Pike, Henry, Dale, Coffee, and Covington.[3] Finally Seddon yielded to the pressure, which had been backed with a strong popular clamor, and wrote the Governor that he might enlist the conscripts as he had requested.[4] Emboldened by this success, the Governor immediately dispatched Colonel Clanton to Richmond

[1] O. R., Ser. 4, Vol. II, pp. 70–71.
[2] Ibid., pp. 253–56.
[3] Ibid., Ser. 1, Vol. LII, Part II, pp. 414–15.
[4] Ibid., see also Montgomery Mail, January 25, 1863.

with a personal letter to the war department asking for all the rest of the conscripts in Alabama who showed any reluctance in going into Confederate service.[1] Judging from later conditions, Clanton evidently met with some success.

Soon after the second conscription act, October, 1862, Governor Brown influenced the Georgia legislature to pass an act providing for a state force to be composed of any of the men not in actual Confederate service.[2] Spoiling, as usual, for a quarrel with President Davis, he wrote the latter that Georgia had a right to every able-bodied man not in actual Confederate service, but that the legislature had adopted the idea of concurrent jurisdiction and had confined its claims to those conscripts not enrolled. He enforced his arguments by a garbled quotation from Davis himself. President Davis had said with reference to the militia: "Congress may call forth the militia to execute Confederate laws. The state has not surrendered the power to call them forth to execute state laws. Con-

[1] O. R., Ser. 4, Vol. II, pp. 419–20.

[2] *Ibid.*, p. 264; *Confederate Records of Georgia*, II, 257–58, 274.

gress may call them forth to repel invasion; so
may the state, for it has expressly reserved this
right . . . . for the power is impliedly reserved
of governing all militia except the part in actual
service of the Confederacy." Certainly Davis
had had no intention of surrendering conscripts
to Brown when he wrote this, but this was
Brown's favorite way of exasperating his antagonist—taking a quotation out of its proper
surroundings and twisting it to suit his own interpretation. He concluded his letter with the
admonition that the President must instruct his
enrolling officers to act accordingly.[1] By 1863 he
had two regiments of regularly enlisted state
troops and was calling out for state defense all
between 18 and 45 not in Confederate service.[2]

The legislature in the state of Louisiana
passed a law on January 3, 1863, drafting all
able-bodied men not in the actual military service of the Confederacy.[3] Immediately the law
was put into operation by General Order No. 8,[4]
and the Confederate government was wheedled

[1] O. R., Ser. 4, Vol. II, pp. 263–64.

[2] See *Confederate Records of Georgia*, II, 447–49, 507–8.

[3] O. R., Ser. 4, Vol. II, pp. 398–99.   [4] *Ibid.*

into allowing conscripts to enter the service of
the state; always "until the emergency is over"
—which of course was never over until the war
was ended. On July 27, 1863, General Ruggles
reported that "the state organizations are composed to a great extent of men subject to conscription . . . . that a mutual understanding
had existed . . . . between the state executive
and the Confederate department commander,
based upon orders of the war department allowing states to retain conscripts in existing state
organizations . . . . which has allowed the state
to absorb most if not all of the conscript material."[1]

By the fall of 1862 Mississippi had a considerable state guard in addition to her active
militia,[2] most of whom had been recruited from
conscript material, either by the consent of the
war department or the district commander.[3] In
December Governor Pettus added further to the
state forces by having the legislature enact a law
drafting for state service all between 16 and

[1] *Ibid.*, p. 677.

[2] *Ibid.*, pp. 178–79; cf. *ibid.*, pp. 16, 17.

[3] *Ibid.*, pp. 677, 759–61, 754.

60 not in the actual service of the Confederacy.[1] In the summer of 1863 Governor Pettus, just as these old state organizations were approaching the termination of their enlistment, obtained further permission to recruit them again for local defense.[2] In November, 1863, these troops were reported to the Governor as numbering about 5,000,[3] five-sixths of whom were between the ages of 18 and 45 and would have been subject to conscription if the state organizations had not absorbed them, frequently with the consent— though ofttimes unwilling—of the war department.[4]

In the fall of 1862 there was a strong flare-up of the feeling in North Carolina that the Confederacy had drafted their state troops and left the state in the lurch in the matter of coast defense. Vance championed the popular discontent and fanned the flames higher. Under his guidance the people began to show distinct signs of unwillingness to leave the state to fight. On

[1] O. R., Ser. 4, Vol. II, p. 249; *ibid.*, Ser. 1, Vol. LII, Part II, p. 453.

[2] *Ibid.*, Ser. 4, Vol. II, pp. 697, 701, 754, 760, 765.

[3] *Ibid.*, pp. 927–36. "(3 regiments, 3 battalions, 10 unattached companies, etc.)"

[4] *Ibid.*, pp. 775–76.

October 25 Vance wrote Davis "that many openly declare they want not another man to leave
the state until provision is made for her own
defense."[1] Not obtaining reinforcements in the
necessary quantities, Vance turned to his legislature, which was very decidedly anti-Davis, and
arraigned the central government on the charge
of bad faith. He had supported conscription, he
said, because he thought he would "actually be
providing for state defense," but he had been
tricked; the citizens of North Carolina had been
taken from their state, leaving her stripped and
defenseless; and despite the fact of her vast, un-
protected seacoast, "she has fewer troops given
her for its defense" than any other state. He
recommended the "raising of at least ten regiments" for state defense.[2] These words fell upon
hungry listeners; the legislature immediately enacted his proposal into a law.[3] Vance then ad-
dressed himself boldly to President Davis asking
for rifles to arm his troops with, and requesting
that he be allowed to enlist all conscripts he had

[1] *Ibid.*, pp. 146–47. This feeling became worse as time passed. See
Jones, *Diary*, I, 303, 325; II, 37.

[2] O. R., Ser. 4, Vol. II, pp. 180–81. [3] *Ibid.*, p. 210.

need of, without interference.[1] Seddon was unable, of course, at this time to supply rifles for state troops, and he told Vance that the President did not feel authorized to relinquish claims to those who were subject to conscription.[2] But Vance did not wait for this reply; he ordered the Military Board of North Carolina to call out the necessary men to fill up the ten regiments. The Board made a clean sweep of able-bodied men, and a large organization was formed.[3] There were a few men in the legislature who were not hostile to the Administration, so they introduced a resolution into the Senate declaring that the military bill raising ten regiments for state defense out of any material at hand was not intended to create a conflict with the Confederate government; but the Senate immediate-

[1] O. R., Ser 4, Vol. II, p. 210; also Jones, *Diary*, I, 198.

[2] O. R., Ser. 4, Vol. II, pp. 225, 226.

[3] *Richmond Examiner* and *Raleigh Standard*, in *Montgomery Mail*, December 6, 1862; *N.C. Regiments*, I, 13, 14, 51–52. North Carolina already had 6 local-defense regiments in Confederate service, besides the Sixty-seventh and Sixty-eighth North Carolina regulars, and this new levy carried the number up to about 17,000. These local-defense troops were usually mustered into Confederate service for limited periods—for state defense—in order to draw Confederate pay, etc. See *Confederate Records of Georgia*, II, 160–65, 173.

ly defeated the resolution by a vote of twenty-seven to five.[1]

Texas, by December, 1862, had a state force of at least 5,000 men.[2] South Carolina seemed to have kept her local defense troops in spite of the conscription law—due to the fact that they had been regularly enlisted as "troops of war" which a state might unquestionably retain in time of war if it insisted on doing so. In May there were 17,000 local-defense troops in the state, and even those who were being recruited for Confederate service were unwilling to leave the state. Among the latter was the Eighteenth South Carolina Regiment.[3] Virginia also was raising a force of about 10,000 in September, 1862.[4]

Thus, state by state, had the local-defense organizations grown up and multiplied until, like the barnacles upon the hulk of a foundering

---

[1] *Richmond Whig*, in *Montgomery Mail*, January 28, 1863.

[2] O. R., Ser. 4, Vol. II, pp. 548–49; *ibid.*, Ser. 1, Vol. XXVI, Part II, pp. 497, 498; Vol. LIII, p. 840; *Montgomery Mail*, December 14, 1862.

[3] *Annual Cyclopaedia* (1862), p. 759; cf. *Mobile Register*, in *Montgomery Mail*, December 12, 1862; *Montgomery Mail*, April 11, 1863; O. R., Ser. 4, Vol. II, pp. 665, 702, 788, 803; *ibid.*, Ser. 1, Vol. XIV, p. 784.

[4] O. R., Ser. 1, Vol. LI, Part II, p. 620.

ship, they threatened to drag the Confederacy down to destruction. Hoping to remove the necessity for state organizations and to divert all able-bodied material absorbed by them into the general service as well as place local defense under Confederate control, Secretary Seddon proposed, June 6, 1863, to the several governors that they organize all the men and boys above and below military age, able to bear arms, into local defense and limited-service companies under Confederate authority. This could be done under acts of Congress of August 21, 1861, and October 13, 1862. However, the Secretary could not be at all sure that the governors of the several states would make any effort to accomplish the proposed object, so he hit upon the alternative of making a requisition of from 5,000 to 10,000 men on each state. These men were to be mustered into Confederate service for six months.[1] The Secretary, as he explained then and several times afterward, had no intention of having the governors raise these troops for six months, but he thought this requisition might be used as a sort of club to induce the formation

[1] O. R., Ser. 4, Vol. II, pp. 580–82; cf. Jones, *Diary*, I, 347–48.

of the proposed Confederate local-defense units.[1] However, Seddon failed to take the proper measure of state rights and state dignity; the governors nearly all, on one pretext or another, made no move to organize the Confederate local-defense troops, but they took advantage of the requisition made upon them to acquire the residue of the able-bodied men for the state forces. Nor did they transfer their troops to the Confederate service for six months.[2] They pursued their customary policy of "loaning" them to the district commander during an emergency.

Governor Vance was a shining example of the governors who neither raised local Confederate troops nor transferred the state troops to the Confederacy. In his proclamation calling for the organization of state volunteers to meet the Secretary's requisition he was very careful to assure the sensitive North Carolinians that "the control and management of these troops raised under this proclamation will be retained

[1] O. R., Ser. 4, Vol. II, pp. 580–82; cf. Jones, *Diary*, I, 347–48.

[2] Probably Texas and Georgia transferred them for six months—only to involve the Confederate government in a quarrel for keeping the troops in the field too long.

43

by the authorities of the state."[1] Not only did he keep the guiding reins over the state troops; he had the audacity to suggest to President Davis that he be given permission to include 1,200 deserters in his organization. They were, he said, willing to come out and "enlist for defense of their state alone." He admitted that "the effect on the army might be injurious," but that did not deter him from asking the privilege, since the Confederate authorities would never be able to get them anyway.[2]

When the requisition was made upon South Carolina she pursued the same policy. Already possessed of a large force in which there were seven conscripts out of every eight men,[3] the state authorities obtained permission from the war department to keep the conscripts "until the exigency was passed."[4] After obtaining this concession the state refused to transfer the troops because it was feared that the Confederate officers would remove those subject to conscription

[1] O. R., Ser. 4, Vol. II, p. 596.

[2] O. R., Ser. 4, Vol. II, p. 674.

[3] Report of C. D. Melton, commandant of conscripts, South Carolina in O. R., Ser. 4, Vol. II, pp. 812–14.

[4] *Ibid.*, pp. 665, 702, 803, 813.

from the state to the Confederate armies, and thus deprive the state of South Carolina of her chief material for local defense. Thus Adjutant General Garlington, who spoke for the Governor, wrote General Thomas Jordan, chief of the staff.[1]

Nor did Mississippi show a different spirit. Instead of turning the able-bodied men of military age over to the Confederacy and helping to recruit the local-defense companies as requested by the Secretary of War, that state only took a firmer grip upon both local defense and her able-bodied population. The state, like North and South Carolina, got permission to retain the conscripts it already had and use others in districts exposed to invasion in making up the troops asked for.[2] Like the two Carolinas, Mississippi also practically refused to muster her troops into Confederate service after she had been allowed to pre-empt the conscripts. Governor Clark well expressed the position of his state in his message to the legislature in November, 1863: "It is not to be expected," he said,

[1] *Ibid.*, p. 702.

[2] *Ibid.*, pp. 677, 697, 701, 754, 759–61.

"that the Confederate troops will be so disposed as to give protection to all portions of this state. They will occupy certain lines and move for defense of certain points as exigency may require"; and he thought like his predecessor Pettus, that "a large force [of state troops] was necessary to our defense." The result was that out of 7,000 troops called for, only about 26 companies of about 1,500[1] were organized under the Confederate law for local defense, and the remainder were either retained entirely by the state or were mustered temporarily into Confederate service.[2]

The reaction of Governor Brown of Georgia toward Seddon's proposition was characteristic. He refused to lift his hand until the Secretary promised not to take any part whatsoever in the direction of the matter. "If the President," he said, "will accept 8,000 men organized by the state . . . . and tendered for six months, ... I think I can have them ready by August the first. If this is satisfactory, say so . . . . and instruct Confederate officers not to attempt to get

[1] O. R., Ser 4, Vol. II, p. 936.
[2] *Ibid.*, pp. 926, 928, 976–78.

up conflicting organizations."[1] Seddon showed a reluctance in forbidding Confederate officers to organize local companies, as it was strictly within their rights under the new law to do so, and Governor Brown instantly washed his hands of the whole affair with the remark that he could do nothing toward organizing troops under Confederate law other than to "invite" men to form themselves into such units.[2] Seeing the futility of attempting to co-operate with Brown, he finally decided to let the Governor handle the whole matter, as the latter much desired. He wrote Brown that if he would undertake the matter so as to obtain the whole number required, that he would agree to leave the organization of the entire outfit in Brown's hands.[3] The result was that Brown made a wonderful showing on paper and advertised his ability to raise troops all over the South. To the Confederate government, however, his energies were of little benefit; the troops he turned over to the war department were nothing but limited-service state troops; very few Confederate local-defense troops were formed.

[1] *Ibid.*, p. 584.
[2] *Ibid.*, pp. 590–91.　　　　[3] *Ibid.*, p. 595.

As soon as Governor Brown had all the concessions he wanted in raising these troops he found fresh ground on which he began a quarrel with the Confederate authorities. After the battle of Chicamauga he thought that the Secretary of War should allow the six-months troops to go home until another big battle was to be fought, in order that they might attend their crops and other duties. His opinion was that the Confederacy had promised to use them only in emergency, and that it was in honor bound to release them when there was no emergency.[1] This was true of the Confederate local-defense troops, but as Brown's stubbornness had resulted in the formation of state troops who had been mustered for six months, this rule did not apply. As a result, Secretary Seddon kept them in continuous service, and Governor Brown's wrath knew no bounds. After haranguing his legislature on the subject,[2] November 13, 1863, he wrote Davis that the Confederate government had broken faith with the Georgia troops, and that as a result of his keeping them in service,

[1] O. R., Ser. 4, Vol. II, p. 824.
[2] *Confederate Records of Georgia*, II, 523–26.

their crops had been ruined. He demanded that they be allowed to go home at once "till another exigency calls for their service."[1] In January, 1864, he again resumed this quarrel and denounced the Confederate authorities for failure to keep faith with "part of the state guard called out early in September last and kept constantly" in the service. He claimed that there was no emergency that demanded their services, and that this act of injustice on the part of the Confederate government had "engendered a feeling which will render it very difficult to enlist another similar force in the state."[2] Seddon's reply was that the military situation had been one of constant emergency—so much so that a "judicial administration did not justify the disbanding of any troops under the control of the department." Seddon also reminded the irate governor that the latter had furnished state troops when the call had really been made for special-service and local-defense Confederate organizations, and that as a result it had been impossible to dismiss and recall them; such organ-

[1] O. R., Ser. 4, Vol. II, pp. 952-53.
[2] *Ibid.*, Vol. III, pp. 61-62; cf. Jones, *Diary*, II, 145-46.

49

izations were too unwieldy for that. Finally, the fault really was Brown's.[1] But Governor Brown was not the man to let anyone else have the last word, so without any delay he shifted the quarrel over to the question as to the kind of troops Seddon had called for in his original proposal, attempting to prove by his usual clever method of making quotations out of their connections that Seddon had simply told a lie when he stated that the original call was for local-defense Confederate troops.[2] But Brown had so many controversies on his hand at this time that it is a marvel to one who has gone over the voluminous correspondence involved how he managed to keep track of them all and remember who his enemies were and what their points of difference were. It really gains us nothing to follow up this particular controversy any farther, as we may safely assume that the Governor never ceased night or day in his waking hours—or perhaps in his dreams—to throw obstacles in the path of the Confederacy.

[1] O. R., Ser. 4, Vol. III, pp. 164–65.

[2] The original proposal of Secretary Seddon shows that he, and not Brown, was right. See *ibid.*, II, 580–82.

After this vain effort to obtain control of the state troops and of local defense, the next step was to draft the state forces into military service of the Confederacy and form them into the "reserves" for state defense. The conscription act of February 17, 1864, had this for its main object. All between seventeen and eighteen, forty-five and fifty were drafted for state defense, and it began to look as if the war department was about to consummate its oft-defeated ideals of a unified and concentrated military system. But once more its *bête noir*, state rights, overthrew its calculations. This time two elements heretofore of minor importance in all the states except Georgia and North Carolina enter upon a prominent rôle in causing the states to retain troops of their own. First was the necessity of retaining as many producers at home as possible in order to relieve the great suffering and want that was being felt all over the South by 1864. Men who belonged to state organizations could be sent home on indefinite furloughs until called out by the governor to meet an emergency, after which they might be furloughed again. This would enable the men to tend their farms and manage their businesses. On the other hand, if a man belonged to the Confederate reserves, he would in all probability be kept in constant service, and his business would go to ruin, his farm grow up in weeds, and those dependent upon his labors would suffer. In the second place, there was a growing sensitiveness on the part of the states as to their constitutional right to maintain "troops of war." Many things had been happening during late years that raised the heretofore mild form of state sovereignty into an active, dangerous type; the Confederacy had long been impressing what it needed with a heavy hand; it was putting men in prison without warrant and executing them, so men said, without trial; provost marshals were requiring the civil population to carry passes miles away from the military lines; the Confederate government had destroyed the state troops in 1862 by conscription; it had attempted to get them in 1863 by a ruse; and now it had drafted them outright—it began to appear, even to otherwise calm, well-balanced men, that the Confederate government was building up a military despotism at the expense of the sovereignty of the state. The party of Stephens-Toombs-Brown-Vance won many new adherents at this point. They all belligerently asserted the constitutional right to maintain "troops of war" in order to preserve the sovereignty and the dignity of the state.

We might safely assert that the greater part of the hostility to conscription, except in Georgia and North Carolina, developed after the passage of the law of February, 1864, and that the hostility was largely due to the fact that the law proposed to divest the states of their right to maintain "troops of war"—the *sine qua non* of their sovereignty.

Governor Clark, of Mississippi, whose state had always been able, without resorting to hostilities with the Confederate government, to retain a force of several thousand was, after the passage of the conscript law of February, 1864, at last confronted with the alternative of an utter abandonment of the state's right to "troops of war" or defiance of the Confederate law. The Governor made inquiries through his friend, Mr. Watson, whether the state would be permitted to retain its troops; and on February 26, Secretary Seddon wrote Governor Clark that the Confederate government laid claim to all men who were not regularly enlisted as "troops of war," and that he considered the Mississippi organizations as nothing but ordinary militia which would be subject to conscription.[1] The Governor now saw that it had been put squarely up to him whether he would insist upon what he considered the rights of the state, or whether he would back down and allow the Confederate government to have his troops. The Governor was not noisy like Brown and Vance. But he quietly insisted on his right to "troops of war," as he called the state organizations, and to any citizen "not actually brought under the authority of the Confederate government,"[2] and kept one of the largest forces heretofore raised for local defense in the state during the spring and summer following the last conscription law.[3] As the year wore on and the Federal armies pressed more and

[1] O. R., Ser. 4, Vol. III, pp. 172–74; cf. *ibid*., pp. 821–22; Jones remarks at this point that it seemed "the states respectively mean to take control of all their men not now in the Confederate-states armies," and that he feared there would be "confusion worse confounded" (Jones, *Diary*, II, 377); cf. *ibid*., I, 199.

[2] O. R., Ser. 4, Vol. III, pp. 903, 904.

[3] *Ibid*., pp. 307–9; *ibid*., Ser. 1, Vol. XXXII, Part III, pp. 650–51.

more into the state, the Governor included yet larger numbers in the state organizations. In September, 1864, he issued a proclamation in which he asserted his right to all persons, without regard to age, if they would enlist in the state forces.[1] The effect of the attitude taken by Governor Clark was the failure of the Confederate government to organize an effective reserve force in Mississippi. General Brandon wrote General Cooper in the fall of 1864 that "the enlistment of men in state organizations had virtually arrested . . . . the . . . . enrolment of the reserves. . . . . All are rushing into the state organizations";[2] and about a month later, in November, he wrote President Davis to the same effect, and added that the men liable to service were going into the state regiments "even after being enrolled."[3] The state forces thus built up at the expense of the Confederate armies, as early as August, 1864, numbered 5,000 enlisted men and 8,000 militia in active service,[4] and as General Brandon had pointed out, there was a

[1] *Ibid.*, Ser. 4, Vol. III, p. 710; cf. *ibid.*, p. 740.

[2] *Ibid.*, p. 740.   [3] *Ibid.*, pp. 823–24.

[4] *Ibid.*, p. 590; *ibid.*, Vol. LII, Part II, p. 726.

great amount of enlistment in the state organizations during the months after August, which must have added very materially to the 13,000 men already reported in active state service. These troops were kept by the state of Mississippi until the war was practically over, when the Governor was finally induced to agree to part with those claimed by the Confederate government.[1]

Governor Watts, of Alabama, who had a considerable organization of local-defense troops when the last conscript law was passed, refused to part with them and allow them to enter the Confederate reserves. His first tilt over this matter happened when he got wind of the fact that the Confederate government was about to conscript a special regiment of young men who held their commissions through the influence of the Governor and who were from the best families of the state and probably very influential. He won a partial victory by forcing the Confederacy to accept them as organized, thus insuring these young officers their commissions, and at the

[1] For the controversy over the surrender of these troops, see O. R., Ser. 4, Vol. III, pp. 902-4, 1162-67; *ibid.*, Ser. 1, Vol. LII, Part II, pp. 810-11.

same time saving his dignity.[1] But the other state organizations he absolutely refused to hand over to the reserve officers. These were composed mostly of men above forty-five who had farms and business interests as well as families, which explained the fact that he refused to let them go when he had allowed the Confederate authorities to take over the regiment of youngsters. In pursuance of his policy of retaining his state forces, Watts became involved in a controversy with the Confederate authorities, who insisted upon their right to all men of military age not exempt by law. On May 31 he wrote Seddon that the enrolling officers were taking his men to camps of instruction for the reserves, and that this was doing great injury to the planting interests. This, he thought, was the "most egregious folly, to call it by no harsher name," he had ever heard of. Not only was it foolish to take "men over forty-five and boys under eighteen from their farms . . . . placing them in camps to do nothing" while their crops were ruining, but it was also an injustice to the men and an encroachment upon the reserved right of the state

[1] *Ibid.*, Ser. 4, Vol. III, pp. 276, 472.

57

to maintain "troops of war." He could see no object the Confederate government could have in taking men out of one local-defense organization and putting them in another "unless it is to prevent any state organization" whatever; and, if this were the case, he said, while he had heretofore confined himself to remonstrance against taking his troops, he might feel himself "justified in going farther unless some stop is put to the matter." He was determined that under no conditions would he "permit the troops organized for state defense . . . . to be taken out of the control of the state."[1]

What was left of Louisiana went busily ahead organizing or continued to keep the state troops already on hand. Attempts were made to prevent the recruiting of these state forces at the expense of the Confederate government, but they proved futile. Preston Pond, who helped the Governor look after the interests of the state, wrote Governor Allen on May 8, 1864, that the

[1] O. R., Ser. 4, Vol. III, pp. 463–64. The Governor sent a few more threatening letters into Richmond (*ibid.*, p. 466), with the result apparently, that he desired. Preston made the remark on receiving one of these letters that the "tendency of the action of the state authorities is to absorb the whole class of reserves" (*ibid.*, p. 464).

Confederate officers of that district had issued an order to prevent the organization of state troops. However, he said, "Major Cockern is proceeding strictly according to law. He came to me for advice and my advice was to disregard all such orders, maintain his organizations, and proceed to complete it [organization] according to law and the orders received from you; that whether the state had the right and power to form troops of her own out of any material she pleased" was not a question to be "settled by any Confederate officer."[1] Governor Allen then protested to the war department that the action of the Confederate government was a personal offense and an insult to the state.[2]

Florida seems to have asserted the state's right to troops rather successfully during the last year of the war. Adjutant General Hugh Archer reported, September 19, 1864, "that there have been organized and commissioned thirty-nine companies of state troops embracing an aggregate of 2,780 men."[3] In Texas during the latter part of 1863 and the first half of 1864 the situa-

---

[1] *Ibid.*, p. 400.

[2] Jones, *Diary*, II, 324. [3] O. R., Ser. 4, Vol. III, p. 669.

tion was about as bad as one could imagine. The large state forces, made up chiefly of conscripts, had been mustered into Confederate service for six months about the middle of 1863,[1] and their term of service had expired by the end of the year. Immediately, General Smith called upon the Governor to let him continue to use these troops, but the latter refused on the ground that the situation was not as bad as General Smith had described, and further, because all the Confederate troops had been sent out of Texas into Louisiana.[2] Governor Murrah was supported in his position on this question by the Texas legislature which passed a law in February, 1864, claiming every conscript in Texas not in actual Confederate service.[3] The Governor thus gained a firm hold upon his troops. He allowed them to reorganize under new officers who were "fixed," and go on detail as wagon-drivers. He flatly refused to listen to the importunities of the Confederate generals of that department to give them succor, although at the time he had 5,000

[1] O. R., Ser. 1, Vol. XXVI, Part II, pp. 497–98.

[2] *Ibid.*, Ser. 1, Vol. XXXV, Part II, pp. 1087–95, 1103.

[3] *Ibid.*, Part III, pp. 786–89.

men who belonged to the state force hauling cotton.[1] However, when half the year had passed, Governor Murrah was finally brought to see the Confederate point of view after General Magruder had threatened to take the conscript material by force, or else to march out of Texas and leave the defense of that state to the Governor's "wagon-drivers."[2] But great hurt had been done the Confederate cause by the time the Governor promised to surrender his organizations. In truth, General Magruder said, Murrah had done more harm to the cause in Texas than the federals by "his factious opposition to the laws of Congress on such grounds as the 'dignity of the state' . . . . and the extreme state-rights construction of the laws of Congress."[3] Magruder pointed out very aptly the effect of such a controversy and a conflict of authority between the Confederate and state authorities. He had "complete and practical evidence that wherever the Confederate authorities and that of the state come into conflict, men unhesitatingly make use

[1] *Ibid.*, p. 726.

[2] *Ibid.*, pp. 786–89.

[3] *Ibid.*, p. 727.

61

of that conflict to avoid military service, and certainly that of the Confederate states." He said that when the Governor of Texas had issued his proclamation claiming all the conscripts according to the state law of February, 1864, "whole brigades disbanded and returned home," and immediately afterward "desertion from the Confederate troops became much more extensive."[1]

In Georgia, as we might have expected, there was a very poor showing made in the matter of organizing the state troops into reserves.[2] Governor Brown, in accordance with a resolution of the legislature, promised not to do anything that would interfere with the law providing for their organization but he paid no attention to this promise. He had already had great success in urging his legislature to appropriate $8,000,000 as a fund to maintain the state troops and to pass new laws reorganizing the militia.[3] So he

[1] O. R., Ser. 1, Vol. XXXV, Part III, pp. 786–89.

[2] The number of reserves raised in Georgia were so few that General Cobb was compelled to use them all in guarding the 30,000 federal prisoners in that state. O. R., Ser. 1, Vol. LII, Part II, pp. 736–40.

[3] *Annual Cyclopaedia* (1863), p. 448; *Confederate Records of Georgia*, II, 601–10.

started the year 1864 with 8,000,[1] and under local stress he added to them as the year wore on.[2]

The war department utterly failed, as a matter of course, to get these troops through the law of February. It then attempted to get Governor Brown to transfer them under a requisition, with the result that it became involved in the bitterest controversy of the whole war. In order to understand this ugly quarrel between the Governor and the Confederate authorities it will be necessary to go back to another controversy— having to do with local defense—that led into this one. In June, 1864, Sherman was striking at the city of Atlanta, and Brown was in a state of frenzy. So on June 28 he wired Davis to send Generals Forrest and Morgan to cut off Sherman's line of communication in order to force his withdrawal or capture. Brown had never shown

---

[1] O. R., Ser. 4, Vol. II, p. 977. Governor Clark referred to this number in his message to the Mississippi legislature as showing what other states were doing in the matter of local defense, and as proof of what Mississippi should do. Cf. *Confederate Records of Georgia*, II, 601–10.

[2] On August 30, 1864, for instance, when Secretary Seddon made his requisition upon Georgia, there were 10,000 organized and others reported as available. O. R., Ser. 1, Vol. LII, Part II, p. 727; cf. *Confederate Records of Georgia*, II, 774–75.

any disposition to go to the aid of other states, but now that Georgia was threatened he demanded that all else must be stopped and reinforcements sent to his state. "This place," he urged Davis, "is to the Confederacy almost as important as the heart is to the human body." It must be held at all odds.[1] On the following day Davis wired Brown that Morgan and Forrest were engaged in a special work and that their services were indispensable in their "present field." Moreover, he assured Brown, "the disparity of forces between the opposing armies in North Georgia is less . . . . than at any other point."[2] This reply to Brown's demands was perfectly courteous, yet on receipt of the telegram the Governor flew into a rage, both on account of Davis' refusal of reinforcements and what he was pleased to regard as an "exhibition of temper" on the part of the President. He dispatched Davis a hot message attacking the Confederate military policy of dispersion, which above all others Brown had foisted upon the Richmond government; and he assured the President that

[1] O. R., Ser. 1, Vol. LII, Part II, pp. 680–81.
[2] *Ibid.*, p. 681.

"if Atlanta is sacrificed and Georgia overrun while our cavalry is engaged in distant raids, you will have no difficulty in finding from correct sources of information what was expected of you."[1]

Receiving no aid from Richmond, the Governor took matters into his own hands; the old quarrel arising over conscription, over his jealousy of the President's power of detail, over the right to "state troops of war," over his claim to detail whom it pleased him, he settled in his favor with a stroke of the pen. He literally made a clean sweep of the political board. By a proclamation declaring that Georgia was abandoned to her own defense he drafted into state forces all the Confederate details—agricultural, mechanical, and industrial, with the exception of those engaged in the Confederate arsenals—unless these details had been countersigned by the state of Georgia; he drafted all Confederate exempts, unless he had also exempted them, members of the Confederate local-defense companies, and all persons subject to military service but not yet actually under Confederate

[1] *Ibid.*, p. 687.

control. On the other hand, he exempted all persons employed in the mills and factories—now working for the state—on the railroads, all policemen, mayors, firemen, guards of the penitentiary, employees of the state armory, and all state-house employees.[1] Thus he took the Confederate details and exempts and left his own unmolested. Those whom the Confederate government had desired to leave at home, he took; those the Confederate government had desired to see in military service, Governor Brown left alone. It was typical of the man. But he must needs add insult to injury: on July 19, a few days after this famous proclamation, he wired the President to instruct his officers to cease "throwing obstacles in the way of getting these men [Confederate details] into active service."[2] Of course Davis did all he could to check the Governor's course in laying claims to Confeder-

[1] O. R., Ser. 1, Vol. LII, Part II, pp. 688–91. Confederate details were obnoxious in Brown's sight; by the law of February, 1864, all men between 17 and 18, and 45–50 had been subject to service in reserve unless "detailed" by the President. Brown regarded this as one of the last moves of Davis to gather complete power over the entire population of Georgia (*Confederate Records of Georgia*, II, 601–10).

[2] O. R., Ser. 1, Vol. LII, Part II, pp. 709–10.

ate details and conscripts. He instructed Seddon that the details must not be allowed to go into Georgia organizations, but that they were subject in emergency "to be ordered out with the reserves."[1] Similar instructions were sent to Howell Cobb, general of reserves in Georgia,[2] and on the same day Brown was notified that the detailed men were in Confederate service and could not be incorporated in the state forces.[3] But these instructions and warnings were all for naught: the Governor went along the course of opposition he had marked out for himself. At length, when he had raised and equipped as many as he wanted, he "loaned" his troops to General Hood—subject always to the condition that he could withdraw them and send them home when he desired.[4] This was a poor makeshift in a crisis like that facing the Confederate armies, for Brown had no better military judgment than to withdraw his militia in the midst of a pitched battle. This was an intolerable situation—a state force, filled with conscripts, exempts, and Confederate details,

[1] *Ibid.*, p. 710. [3] *Ibid.*, p. 711.
[2] *Ibid.* [4] *Ibid.*, pp. 717, 724, 725.

liable at any moment, without notice, to be withdrawn from service. If only they could be mustered into Confederate service, the tangled thread could be straightened: the details could be transferred to the reserves, where they really belonged, the exempts could be sent home, the conscripts put in general service, and the details Brown had made, put back in the militia; and the troops would be subject—not to the whims of a suspicious and vindictive governor—but to the orders of a Confederate general. Hence, on August 30 Seddon made a requisition upon the Governor for his 10,000 militia, hoping thus to settle the matter.[1]

But the very thing that the Confederate authorities had planned to prevent now happened: as if to anticipate the requisition Brown sent his troops home on a thirty-day furlough, during the most critical moments of the campaign around Atlanta. This was simply a maneuver in local politics—the Governor was taking care to mend his fences even while Atlanta was falling into the hands of the enemy. In his proclamation the Governor praised the troops

[1] O. R., Ser. 1, Vol. LII, Part II, p. 727.

for their service and gallantry, and told them
that it was their due, as the emergency was over,
that opportunity be given them to put their
houses in order and take a breathing spell.[1] Two
days after sending the troops home to rest,
Brown received the requisition from Seddon.
Without a doubt the Governor was the angriest
and bitterest person on the continent at the
moment. With his pen fairly reeking with gall
he wrote the Secretary a flat, unconditional refusal. The President, he said, had scattered his
forces "from Texas to Pennsylvania while a
severe blow was being struck at the heart of the
Confederacy"; and that with 30,000 men lying
idle in Texas, and the reserves guarding prisoners
back of the lines, he had refused to send a man
to reinforce the Confederate army defending
Atlanta. If the President had had control of the
militia, he said, in all probability he would have
sent it to some other state to fight, or he would
have disbanded and placed over it "his own pár-
tisans and favorites." But most important of
all, Brown actually feared that the requisition
for his militia was a move on the part of Davis,

[1] *Ibid.* pp. 735-36. Cf. Jones, *Diary*, II, 311.

whom he already regarded as a regular Nero, to disarm Georgia so as to prevent resistance to further encroachments on her reserved rights. He would refuse to "gratify the President's ambition . . . . and surrender the last vestige of the sovereignty of the state."[1]

On October 8, Seddon refuted Brown's unjust accusations against the motive of the President in making the requisition. There were two motives, he said, in making the requisition. In the first place, it was desired to put the state troops under the control of the Confederate generals, where they would be relied upon at all times. For "it is easy," he wrote, "to see how uncertainty as to their control or retention must impair reliance by the commander on these troops, and embarrass all calculations for their employment and efficiency in combined operations." The second reason had been that the troops requisitioned contained conscripts and Confederate details "which had engendered controversy

[1] O. R., Ser. 1, Vol. LII, Part II, pp. 736–40. Cf. Jones, *Diary*, II, 292. Brown's opposition to the law of February, 1864, conscripting all between 17–18, 45–50 for service in the Confederate reserve was largely an outgrowth of the fear that Davis was attempting to deprive Georgia of her militia and thus deny her right to "troops of war" (*Confederate Records of Georgia*, II, 601–10).

and endangered collision between the local Confederate and state authorities" which it was thought might be terminated by gaining control over the troops. The Secretary then accused Brown of playing into the hands of the enemy, who believed from his words and actions that he was prepared to "entertain overtures of separate accommodation." He arraigned him for refusing to obey the provision of the Constitution that made the President commander in chief of all the military forces. This, he pointed out, was a repetition of what Massachusetts and Connecticut had done during the War of 1812, which had resulted in casting a shadow over the loyalty of those states.[1] Brown's reply to this letter again accused the President of aiming at absolute power by grasping into his hands the entire control of the Confederate and state forces. As to the President's attempt to settle the quarrel over the details and conscripts in the state force by requisition, Brown sarcastically remarked that it was a "new discovery of the President of the mode of settling a controverted right," by which the stronger took from the weaker, "and

[1] O. R., Ser. 1, Vol. LII, Part II, pp. 754-58.

the magnanimity and statesmanship displayed by him in this affair cannot be too highly appreciated." He flatly denied that the President was commander in chief of the militia, except when it was actually in Confederate service, with the power to call it out at his discretion.[1] Seddon immediately cited the Confederate laws of February 28 and March 6, 1861, that conferred plenary power upon the President to employ all military forces of the Confederate states, including militia, the regular army, or any other forces organized in the Confederacy. "In my judgment," said he, "these acts . . . . bind you both as a citizen and an officer, and you owe prompt, cordial, and unhesitating obedience to them."[2] Brown's rejoinder was that the acts were not susceptible to any such construction, but that if, as Seddon contended, they were, then "Congress had no power or authority to pass them."[3]

The argument had lasted six months, but it had booted the Confederate government noth-

[1] O. R., Ser. 1, Vol. LII, Part II, pp. 778–90.

[2] *Ibid.*, pp. 796–99.

[3] *Ibid.*, pp. 803–7.

ing. Brown kept the state troops and all the Confederate details; as late as March 13, 1865, when it was all about over, Governor Brown issued the following defiant order: "All persons belonging to Major Smith's division are in the actual military service of the state. No one of them, whether detailed agriculturists [Confederate] or not, will obey any order from a Confederate officer. . . . . The Confederate officers can take no control over them without the consent of the state till they are disbanded by the state. They are now on furlough."[1]

Having failed to get control of the state forces by all the methods heretofore tried, President Davis turned in despair to the Confederate Congress and asked them to pass a law that would enable him to take them over in a body by some form of requisition.[2] But Congress by this time

---

[1] *Ibid.*, Ser. 4, Vol. III, p. 1138. In the controversy that lasted from July 16, 1864, to January, 1865, the Confederate authorities had finally, when they were seeking an honorable surrender to Brown, consented that conscripts and details might remain in Brown's militia until the militia was disbanded. The result of such a promise was that Brown never disbanded his militia, but sent them home on indefinite furloughs, thereby preventing the Confederate government from asserting its claims over them.

[2] *Ibid.*, p. 1133; *Journal of the Confederate Congress*, IV, 704-5.

was dominated by the idea of state rights and state sovereignty. Brown, Stephens, Toombs, Vance, Rhett, Pollard, and their like, and not Davis, were the leaders to whom Congress now looked for inspiration. His appeal fell upon deaf ears. The Committee on Military Affairs reported that it was their opinion that any law transferring the control of the state troops to the President would in reality be equivalent to another conscription act, which they were not willing to adopt.[1]

In retrospect, we see that the states were so strongly imbued with the idea of their own separate identity and rights that they attempted their own defense. This resulted in withdrawing arms from general service during the first year of the war, when the Confederate government was unable to obtain an adequate supply elsewhere, and thereby prevented the recruiting of the Confederate armies; it resulted, especially after the first year, when arms were more plentiful, in withdrawing large numbers of men from the general service. The attempts of the Confederate government to obtain control of the

[1] O. R., Ser. 4, Vol. III, pp. 1145-46.

men and arms thus "sidetracked" aroused many
bitter feuds between the state and Confederate
authorities. Altogether, local defense contributed very materially to the defeat of the Confederacy.

CHAPTER II

RELATION OF THE STATES TO THEIR TROOPS IN THE CONFEDERATE SERVICE

If the states insisted upon the right to have their own troops of war for local defense, they also demonstrated their sovereignty by asserting more or less successfully certain claims over their troops in the Confederate service: (*a*) in the first place the states, each, until conscription was adopted, insisted that all troops coming from within its borders must be tendered to the Confederate government through the governor or other state agent; (*b*) most of the states in one way or other insisted upon the right to appoint officers over their troops in Confederate service; and (*c*) many of the states, instead of pooling their resources, attempted to supply their own troops, thereby taking the matter as far as possible out of the hands of the Confederate government.

76

I. INDEPENDENT ACCEPTANCE

The exasperating laggardliness of the states in sending forward troops, the eternal quibbling, the inevitable interpretation of the orders from the war department by the state authorities, soon convinced the Confederate government that it must open another channel beside that of the state through which the enthusiastic population might be brought into military service. There was only one way practicable at this time, and that was to allow direct volunteering into the Confederate armies without the formality of passing through the hands of the governor or other state authorities. This was done, and as we have already seen, 200,000 men more than the Confederacy could arm offered their services at once.[1] We will also recall that the Confederate government was unable to arm them because the states held back the necessary arms for the purpose of local defense. However, in retaining these arms there was an element of spite involved, for the states refused to arm the direct volunteers because they objected to the Confederacy's raising troops outside of the state

[1] See p. 22.

agency. As a result of this state sensitiveness to independent acceptance there arose quite a controversy with the central government.

The policy of "independent acceptance" met with instant opposition in Georgia. The state was barely settled down as a member of the Confederacy and war had not opened before Governor Brown dispatched an ultimatum to Secretary Walker against direct volunteering. He warned the Secretary not to accept or call out troops in Georgia except through requisition on her Governor. He might be better acquainted than the Secretary, he remarked sarcastically, "with the best selection of the companies for the service."[1] The war department continued, however, to accept men who had arms, regardless of the Governor's complaints. Thereupon Brown, who knew that the Confederacy had nothing with which to arm these men, ordered all direct volunteers to leave their arms behind on marching out of the state.[2] This, he was sure, would stop the practice more effectively than his protests to the Confederate government. Walker

[1] O. R., Ser. 4, Vol. I, p. 215.
[2] See p. 16 above; O. R., Ser. 1, Vol. LII, Part II, p. 97.

immediately remonstrated against Brown's interference, telling him that the law permitting direct volunteering had been enacted to prevent the delay caused by the states, and that Brown was simply defeating the law by his attitude.[1] Brown promptly wired the Secretary that he regarded the law permitting tender of troops independent of state authority as "a very dangerous infringement of state rights," and that he was unwilling to help in the raising of troops under its terms.[2] Seeing that Walker had no intentions of receding from his position and that the regiments of direct volunteers were attempting to carry their arms out of the state in disobedience to his orders, Brown carried the matter to the President. He demanded that he direct "Colonels Connor and Brumby and other colonels whose regiments were accepted under direct tender," to obey the Governor's orders about leaving their guns.[3] However, a few of these companies managed to elude the watchful Brown and get out of Georgia into Virginia with the prohibited state rifles before he got wind of what

[1] O. R., Ser. 4, Vol. I, p. 332.
[2] *Ibid.* [3] *Ibid.*, p. 366.

was happening. But if they thought they had put one over on the Governor, he promptly showed them they were laboring under a mistake. Seven or eight hundred miles and over-crowded transportation were a trifling matter when the Governor was threatened with losing a point in an argument with the Confederate government. He wired Davis a demand that the arms be returned "by express to Atlanta immediately."[1] He was determined to stop independent acceptance or break up the Confederacy.

In accepting volunteers in this fashion, the war department encountered opposition in Louisiana. Governor Moore wrote the Secretary that he was both surprised and hurt that the Confederate government should grant permission for individuals to raise troops without consulting him. He thought that troops should be raised only through requisition upon the Governor. Not only did courtesy require it, but he was of the opinion that efficiency demanded it. He felt sure that the attempts to raise organizations outside of those required of the state as its quota

[1] O. R. Ser. 4, Vol. I, p. 401.

would cause confusion and defeat the efforts of both the state and the representatives of the Confederate government in raising troops.[1] A few months later, about the middle of July, 1861, Governor Moore entered another protest against the war department's thus overreaching the Governor of a state. It interfered, he wrote, very materially with the efforts of the state to fill quotas. In fact, he was sure that Louisiana would be unable to meet the requisitions of the central government unless the Secretary of War should revoke all authority granted certain individuals in that state to raise volunteers for direct tender.[2] Failing to get the orders he wanted from Richmond, Moore, like Brown and the other governors, put a check on these organizations by refusing to arm them.[3]

Governor Clark, of North Carolina, objected on similar grounds: it interfered, he said, with the filling of the state's quota; it was overreaching the governor and compromising the dignity of the state.[4] Governor Pickens protested against the arming of these independent regi-

[1] *Ibid.*, pp. 194–95.
[2] *Ibid.*, pp. 444–45.
[3] *Ibid.*, p. 336.
[4] *Ibid.*, p. 987.

ments when he had 4,400 men, just raised by state authority to fill a requisition from the war department, all without proper arms.[1] This was putting individuals upon a better footing than the state of South Carolina.

Due to the very pronounced policy of Texas of keeping her troops for her own defense, the Confederate government gave rather free rein in that state to men of energy and influence in raising Confederate volunteers. In November Governor Clark, in his message to the legislature, assailed this as being both unwise and unjust. It had been most emphatically objected to, he complained, but to no purpose. He thought it only right that the "state executive should at least be officially informed" when permission was given to these individuals to raise independent regiments.[2] But the state continued to move slowly in meeting its quotas. So the war department deemed it best to increase the independent organizations rather than decrease them, with the result that in the spring of 1862 Governor Lubbock, who had succeeded Clark,

[1] O. R., Ser. 4, Vol. I, pp. 634–35.

[2] Ibid., pp. 717–18.

found one man, S. A. Roberts, authorized by the war department to raise five regiments "without consulting with, or reporting in any way to, the authorities of this state."[1] The Governor promptly wrote the Secretary of War that he respectfully demurred and protested "against the government's taking the men out of the state except by call through the state authorities."[2] A few days later he again wrote the Secretary of War that the effect of permitting independent volunteering would be to defeat the effort of the state to raise troops; unless action was taken at once against it, the Governor protested, he would "not be responsible for the time and manner in which Texas fills the requisition made upon her."[3] He followed this letter up by two more in quick succession in which he complained that he continued to learn of others who had been authorized to raise large bodies of troops without his authority.[4] Such a violent bombardment as this was more than the Confederate government could stand. On April 8, 1862, the Secretary of War promised the Governor that in

[1] *Ibid.*, pp. 977, 995.
[2] *Ibid.*, pp. 977–79.
[3] *Ibid.*, p. 995.
[4] *Ibid.*, pp. 1001–2, 1006.

the future all individuals who desired to raise troops must first obtain the consent of the governor before authority would be granted them at Richmond [1] However, the conscript law, passed a few days later, really made the promise to refrain from independent acceptance unnecessary, since it entirely obviated such methods of getting troops.

Arkansas was no less sensitive as to its rights and dignity. Governor Rector had already expressed some objections,[2] but on September 30, 1861, he gave vent to all his wrath against the policy of raising troops without the consent of the state. The occasion of this outbreak was the proclamation of General McCulloch calling for 10,000 volunteers from Arkansas. The proclamation was issued directy to the people of the state, without the sanction of the Governor, and it seemed to Rector nothing short of an insult to Arkansas and an infringement upon the Confederate Constitution. He protested vigorously against what, in his opinion, was a high-handed act of usurpation. His idea, he said, of the rights relatively belonging to the states and to the

[1] O. R., Ser. 4, Vol. I, p. 1051.   [2] *Ibid.*, p. 561.

Confederate government was that "those pertaining to the former were by no means abridged by the withdrawal from the old confederacy and a union with the new government, but that all theretofore claimed upon the most liberal construction were conceded both upon policy and principles." He knew of no precedent in the history of the United States for the raising of troops by proclamation of either the general commanding the department, or the president. Nor did he know of a Confederate law permitting it, but if there was such a law, he said, that "trenched so far upon state prerogative as to authorize the calling of troops by any but state authority," he would very "reluctantly yield" his assent to "so serious an innovation of state rights."[1]

On April 15, 1862, Confederate General Order No. 23 revoked all authority to raise independent commands, which, together with the conscript law passed about the same time, put an end to the controversies over direct tender of troops to the Richmond government.[2]

[1] *Ibid.*, Ser. 1, Vol. III, p. 710.

[2] *Ibid.*, Ser. 4, Vol. I, p. 1059.

2. RIGHT TO APPOINT OFFICERS OF STATE REGIMENTS IN CONFEDERATE SERVICE

The states guarded jealously all their rights of appointment in the army. Their dignity and sovereignty required this; the political success of the governor depended upon it, and local pride and local patriotism demanded it. There were three fairly distinct phases of the question of appointment to the Confederate army offices: there were the attempts to force the Confederacy to accept "skeleton" regiments and organizations larger than regiments in order to force upon the war department officers higher in rank than the Confederate law[1] allowed the states to appoint, as well as to find a berth for favorites of the governor; there was a determined effort in some states to have only citizens of the state appointed to officer the state's troops in Confederate service or to manage conscription; and finally some of the states asserted the right to fill vacancies that occurred among their Confederate officers.

In raising troops for the Confederate service

---

[1] The law allowed the state to appoint officers up to and including the rank of colonel.

in the spring and summer of 1861, the states usually commissioned all the officers from colonel down to second lieutenant and depended upon these favorites to recruit the ranks as best they could. But the Confederate government was pressing the governors for troops and could not calmly wait for these skeleton regiments to be filled. It insisted upon the states' sending forward the small units as soon as filled instead of waiting upon the recruiting of entire regiments. This would have thrown many officers out of commission and would have left the organization of the regiments and the appointment of regimental officers in the hands of the Confederate government. Few governors could deny themselves to such an extent; they either refused to send the troops forward until the entire regiment was recruited, or offered skeleton regiments— ofttimes composed of a colonel, eight or ten captains, thirty or forty lieutenants, and a small sprinkling of privates.

On March 9, 1861, Secretary Walker called upon Governor Brown for 2,000 men to be sent immediately to Pensacola.[1] Three days later the

[1] O. R., Ser. 4, Vol. I, p. 135.

Governor countered by offering him two regiments fully officered, but without the full quota of men in the ranks. There were, he said, only "about 200 enlisted for one regiment and 250 for the other." He wanted the Secretary to permit the officers not actually needed to remain in Georgia to finish recruiting the ranks until the regiments had the required number. He did not feel that he could, with justice to the privates who had enlisted under these officers, tender the regiments unless all the officers were accepted along with them. He was sure that the skeleton regiments could soon be recruited to their full strength.[1] On March 15 Walker replied that he could not accept any such arrangement; that the government had no legal authority to receive fragments and "officers without command."[2] But Robert Toombs, who was in Georgia at this time, came to the rescue of the Governor. He wired the Secretary that the regiments had been raised under an ordinance of the state convention and that the Confederate government

[1] O. R., Ser. 4, Vol. I, pp. 149–50. A regiment had from 800 to 1,000 troops.

[2] *Ibid.*, pp. 166–67.

should accept them under Brown's conditions
and let the officers recruit them to full strength
later.[1] Walker wired him the next day, March
22, that there was no law "to receive fractions
.... to be afterward completed."[2] Toombs,
who had taken the Governor's part entirely by
this time, replied that nothing could be done
except on the basis of Brown's proposal.[3] The
same day the Georgia convention added its
weight to Joe Brown's demands. It resolved that
the President "be requested to receive into the
service .... all the men now enlisted, with the
officers necessary to command them, by companies or battalions, and the remainder of the
force as they may be received with their officers,
until each of the two regiments now being raised
is completed, when the whole force with their
officers shall form as regiments."[4] This was a
slight modification of Brown's first proposition,
as it did not ask that officers without command
be mustered into Confederate service until a
command had been raised for them. Otherwise
it was the same: it would pledge the Confeder-

[1] *Ibid.*, p. 181.   [3] *Ibid.*
[2] *Ibid.*, p. 184.   [4] *Ibid.*, p. 185.

ate government to receive fragments later to be assembled into regiments officered by Brown. Walker, though he was compelled to stretch the Confederate law, seems to have accepted this arrangement, and Brown had won his first contest with the war department.[1]

Nor was Louisiana willing to yield any of the appointments over her troops in the Confederate service. On March 30, 1861, Governor Moore informed Walker that he had been led to believe that "unless the men are mustered by regiments the field officers will not be recognized," and that he had issued an order that no regiments should be transferred till they were completed.[2]

Governor Pickens, of South Carolina, wrote Walker that none of the South Carolina regiments were full, but that he was sending them forward in fragments "with the condition annexed . . . . that the regiments shall not be broken up," but should be assembled and made into full regiments under the regimental officers appointed by the state.[3]

Still another way of imposing state appoint-

[1] O. R., Ser. 4, Vol. I, pp. 191, 192, 193.
[2] Ibid., p. 194.   [3] Ibid., Ser. 1, Vol. I, p. 236.

ments upon the Confederate government was by tendering organizations larger than a regiment, which would carry with them field, staff, and general officers. The Confederate law did not recognize the right of a state to organize units larger than a regiment, reserving the higher organizations for the central government, along with the appointment of field, staff, and general officers. There is no doubt, however, that all the governors would have welcomed the privilege of appointing over the troops that left their state officers from captain to lieutenant general. But none of them, except Governor Brown, actually stood out for this power of appointment as a reserved right of the state. That individual had the habit of getting his legislature to enact laws that were at cross-purposes with the Confederate laws, whereupon he invariably posed as being "bound by law" to pursue his course. In this particular case he had managed to get the legislature to enact a law providing for the organization of an entire brigade. On June 20, 1861, he offered the brigade to Walker, completely organized and officered, as part of Georgia's quota. In making the tender, he mentioned the fact that

it had been "organized under an act of our legislature," thus assuming the attitude as one only
carrying to out the law of his state.[1] Hoping to get
the Governor to surrender his brigade in regiments, according to the Confederate law, Walker
made a requisition on him for two regiments. On
July 8 Brown again offered the whole brigade.
He wrote Walker that he wanted the whole
brigade to enter service as it had been equipped,
with General Phillips in command; but if the
law did not allow the acceptance of whole brigades, he had a way in mind by which Walker
might easily evade the spirit of the law and yet
meet its technicalities: he proposed that he receive the brigade by regiments and then appoint
General Phillips to command it. As an induce-
ment to accept this arrangement, Brown offered
Walker a tempting bribe: he promised him "that
at any cost of labor or expense" to himself or the
state he would furnish two other regiments beside the brigade, as fully armed and equipped as
any that had gone from Georgia.[2] He reminded

[1] O. R., Ser. 4, Vol. I, p. 408.

[2] Here is evidence that Brown had arms if he really had desired to
give them to the Confederacy.

Walker that it really was equivalent to "an offer
to furnish . . . . five regiments."[1] On July 12
Walker wired Brown that the President had no
authority to accept a brigade, and he begged him
for the sake of the cause and the country not to
insist upon the brigade organization, but to send
it forward by regiments as quickly as possible.
"The crisis of our fate," he said, "may depend
upon your action."[2] On July 14 Brown replied
that he did not feel authorized by the state law
to allow the brigade to be broken into regiments
in order to muster it into Confederate service.
Though he felt unauthorized to violate the
Georgia law, he again suggested how Walker
might evade the Confederate law against accepting units larger than regiments "by commission-
ing the general now in command."[3] Two days
later Walker renewed the appeal.[4] Brown then
delayed another half-month with this well-
equipped brigade lying idle at a time—during
the first Manassas campaign—when it might
have changed the history of the Confederacy,
and then very ungraciously yielded to Walker's

---

[1] O. R., Ser. 4, Vol. I, p. 424.   [3] *Ibid.*, p. 477.

[2] *Ibid.*, p. 466.   [4] *Ibid.*, pp. 480–81.

entreaties.[1] For the sake of controlling the appointment of a brigadier general and his aide, Brown had kept from the field during a whole month a well-armed brigade.

Involving only one or two states, but intensely bitter and far-reaching in its ultimate consequence was the conflict over the appointment of resident officers for Confederate service.[2] North Carolina showed the greatest sensitiveness on this point. She furnished few of the great leaders of the war, and Governor Vance, who was quick to sense political fuel, was not slow in laying the blame on the President. He had the feeling that North Carolina was being purposely slighted because that state had shown a reluctance in leaving the Union. He spread this opinion far and wide and aroused a great deal of resentment and discontent in his state, which was all too ready to believe what he said against the Confederate government. In his message to the legislature in the fall of 1862 he

[1] O. R., Ser. 4, Vol. I, p. 527; see also *Confederate Records of Georgia*, II, 91–92, for controversy.

[2] The appointment of commissary agents not residents of a state was a sensitive point. See Jones, *Diary*, Vol. II.

recurred to the fact that "entire brigades of North Carolina soldiers in the field" were commanded by strangers, and that the officers from North Carolina had been set aside to give place to those from other states. This, he said, was fast breaking down the pride and patience of the North Carolina officers, many of whom had expressed their intention to resign because honorable promotion was seemingly closed to them. This was a great wrong, Vance thought, and furnished "just cause of complaint" in the army and at home.[1] This was not all; on January 26, 1863, Vance wrote Seddon that the Confederate government was actually appointing citizens of other states to important offices within North Carolina. A particular case was that of Colonel August, who had been appointed over the heads of many deserving North Carolinians to the rather delicate position of commandant of conscripts for the state. This, said the Governor, really amounted to an official announcement "that North Carolina has no man in her borders fit to command her own conscripts," although there were large numbers of her best officers at

[1] O. R., Ser. 4, Vol. II, p. 189.

home with mutilated limbs and broken health. The people were justly mortified in seeing a stranger brought in to execute an odious law, and he felt that "it smacks of discourtesy, to say the least of it." It was a very impolitic thing to do, and it was his duty, he said angrily, "to inform you that if persisted in, the appointment of strangers to all the positions in the state and over her troops will cause a feeling throughout her borders which it is my great desire to avoid."[1] Following hot upon his letter came the North Carolina delegation in Congress, who urged the change of commandant of conscripts at once. Acting Superintendent of Conscripts Rains, himself a native of North Carolina, assured them that no intentional discrimination had been made; that there had been no available citizen of the state, of proper rank, who was disabled too much for active service and who was not too much disabled for conscript service. He requested them to help find the proper man, whereupon

[1] O. R., Ser. 4, Vol. II, p. 375; see also Jones, *Diary*, I, 249. Jones remarks that "the War Department has erred in putting so many strangers in command of localities where natives might have been selected. Richmond has never yet been in command of a Southern general."

he would willingly remove Colonel August.[1] At length the proper man was located, and Rains notified Governor Vance that Peter Mallet was to take Colonel August's place.[2]

Although Colonel August was important, he was only one officer removed; scores remained to vex the pride of the toucheous Tar Heel State. So in the fall of 1863 Vance took the matter up to engage in another tilt with the Confederate government. Getting results too slowly at a distance, he presently journeyed to Richmond in person and laid the matter before the President. Davis expressed himself as willing to remove the obnoxious "strangers" from the presence of the North Carolinians, whereupon Vance gave him the names of six who demanded immediate attention. However, the President, with the burdens of the war on his frail shoulders, had moved too slowly again to please the Governor, so on September 23, Vance wrote Seddon a letter filled with stinging reproaches. He said the President had not fulfilled his promise in removing the six men, that "neither these men nor any others have been disturbed." At a time when he

[1] O. R., Ser. 4, Vol. II, pp. 411–12.   [2] *Ibid.*, p. 458.

had been striving with all his power to apologize for such appointments and reconcile the people to the unpopular administration, the refusal of such a small favor filled him with disgust. "If I have not sufficient influence with the President," he said hotly, "to secure the removal of one man, ... for God's sake let me know it."[1]

But the most important controversy concerning the appointment of officers was over the right of the governors to fill vacancies among their troops in Confederate service. In raising and organizing its troops for the Confederate armies during the period before conscription, each state always appointed all officers up to and including the rank of colonel. This right was recognized by the Confederate laws.[2] However, once these troops were mustered into the Confederate service, they became part of the army, whose officers, like those of any other department, were subject to the appointment of that government. But this matter of appointment was not perfectly clear at first, even to the Secre-

[1] O. R. Ser., 4, Vol. II, pp. 787–88; also Jones, *Diary*, II, 4, 25, 39.
[2] O. R., Ser. 4, Vol. I, pp. 117, 126, 127.

tary of War[1] and the Attorney-General, for Benjamin ruled in August 1861, that all troops tendered by the state were state militia, subject under the Constitution and laws of the Confederacy to be officered by the state.[2] So it appears that the states filled all vacant offices among their troops in Confederate service during a great part of the first year with the sanction of the War Department and the Department of Justice. However, there were those who saw the vast amount of evil flowing from such arrangements, so in the reorganization of the twelve-months men,[3] and in the conscription act,[4] the Confederate government assumed its rightful power of appointing to all vacancies in its armies; and Attorney-General Watts submitted an opinion that regardless of specific laws these troops were part of the Confederate army, and not militia, and as such were subject to have their vacant offices filled by the central government.[5]

[1] *Ibid.*, pp. 608–9.   [2] *Ibid.*, Vol. III, pp. 655–56.

[3] Benjamin's opinion to Governor Brown, O. R., Ser. 4, Vol. I, pp. 942–43.

[4] *Ibid.*, Vol. II, pp. 610–11. Seddon's opinion to Brown, for conscript law, see *ibid.*, Vol. I, pp. 1095–97.

[5] *Ibid.*, Ser. 4, Vol. III, pp. 655–56.

This reversal of policy met with immediate and serious opposition. In his address to the assembly in November, 1862, Vance conceded that the right to officer the twelve-months troops and the conscript troops had been surrendered to the Confederate government. There were, however, a large body of troops that did not fall within these classes, so the Governor thought: the troops raised and tendered by the state for the entire war. These North Carolina still had a right to control in the matter of granting commissions. As a matter of fact, Vance said that North Carolina, if it desired, had the right to assume the appointing power over the troops included in the conscript and twelve-months organizations.[1] The Governor did not insist upon the right of appointment except among the troops tendered for the war. In the cases of this class, however, in spite of the law and opinion of the Attorney-General, Vance continued to appoint and commission officers until the war was nearly over. Finally, General Cooper notified him that he would recognize no more commissions issued from North Carolina.[2] Vance did

[1] O. R., Ser. 4, Vol. II, p. 189.   [2] *Ibid.*, Vol. III, p. 616.

not acquiesce in this withdrawal of a long-standing privilege without a struggle. He submitted the matter to Attorney-General Davis for an opinion. The change was breeding confusion, he said, and was likely to cause much dissatisfaction. The officers of the troops had been commissioned by the Governor by virtue of an ordinance of the North Carolina convention, and he would like to know whence the President derived his authority to grant commissions over the same troops.[1] Attorney-General Davis explained that the right to appoint officers over the troops in question was derived from a higher source than any specific law: that the Constitution gave the President a right, and also made it obligatory upon him, to appoint the officers. There were, said he, only two kinds of troops, militia and the army of the Confederate states. The Constitution reserved to the states the right to appoint all militia officers, but it also required the President, with the advice and consent of the Senate, to appoint all officers of the army. The question was, in what class did the North Carolina troops referred to fall? That, he said, had

[1] *Ibid.*

already been decided by Attorney-General Watts in August, 1862, and the decision had been "that such troops are a part of the army of the Confederate states." This view had been adopted by the Secretary of War, who felt that he "had no discretion any longer to acquiesce in an arrangement made by his predecessor" under an erroneous construction of the law[1] Although Vance was not at all pleased with the opinion of the Attorney-General and the determined attitude of the war department, he was forced to acquiesce in the Confederate government's making the appointments, and to confine himself to anti-government speeches and letters on the subject.

South Carolina appointed to vacancies among her troops in the Confederate service during the first year of the war, and the reversal of the Richmond government's policy aroused some discontent in official circles. James Chestnut, Jr., chief of the military department, complained to the Governor and Executive Council, in his report of February 16, 1862, that the Confederate government, by a recent ruling, was refusing

[1] O. R., Ser. 4, Vol. III, pp. 655–56.

to allow the state to officer her troops, and he was certain that the right was one which belonged to the state.[1] The complaint was laid before the war department, and as no response was made, the state continued to appoint to the vacancies.[2] At length the war department announced to the South Carolina authorities its intentions to fill all such vacancies. This brought a response from Chestnut, who again urged the matter upon the Secretary of War "with a view to prevent conflict."[3] However, it seems that South Carolina did not insist upon her rights so strongly as North Carolina had.

Virginia[4] and Alabama[5] showed a similar desire to appoint to vacancies among the Confederate troops, and of course Governor Brown never willingly conceded the right of the Confederate government to officer any of Georgia's troops. His first conflict with the Confederate government on this point came as a result of the law to re-inlist the twelve-months men. They had been organized by the states and their officers held

[1] *Ibid.*, Vol. I, p. 916.

[2] *Ibid.*, pp. 1088–89.

[3] *Ibid.*

[4] *Ibid.*, pp. 601–2, 604–5, 609–11.

[5] *Ibid.*, pp. 608–9.

their commissions under state grant. So as soon as Brown heard that the law had been passed to re-inlist and reorganize them, he demanded to know at once whether he or the President was to commission the officers. He wanted to know what the war department and the President understood by the phrase in the Confederate Constitution "reserving to the states respectively the appointment of the officers." This, of course, was a sly way of notifying the Confederate government that he considered himself as having a constitutional right to commission the officers in the reorganized Georgia troops. He assured the Secretary of War, at the same time, that it was his desire, "in the eventful period of our history, to avoid all conflict between the state and the Confederate government."[1] About two weeks later, on February 16, 1862, Benjamin replied that the twelve-months troops who were to be reorganized would have their officers appointed by the President. As to the clause Brown had quoted him, he had no doubt in his mind but that it referred to militia.[2] "Yielding to superior force," Brown dropped the matter of the twelve-

[1] O. R., Ser. 4, Vol. I, pp. 909-10.   [2] Ibid., pp. 942-43.

months men. But he continued to assert his right to fill vacancies in the regiments raised by Georgia "for the war"[1] which resulted in a collision with the Confederate government. In the spring of 1863 the Confederate government appointed an officer to fill a vacancy in the Fifty-first Georgia Regiment. Brown protested, and Seddon pointed out the laws of April 16 and 21, 1862, which provided that all vacancies should be filled by the President. The Secretary regretted very much "that this difference of opinion should have existed," and that the expression of the Governor's opinions should "have been given such direction as may possibly excite much dissatisfaction among the officers of the gallant regiment."[2] Brown's reply to Seddon's citation of Confederate law was that, while the latter based the right of the Confederate states to commission officers upon an act of Congress, he, the Governor of Georgia, based his right to commission them upon the Constitution, and that the act of Congress was in conflict with the Constitu-

[1] *Confederate Records of Georgia*, II, 335–44.

[2] O. R., Ser. 4, Vol. II, p. 611; cf. *Confederate Records of Georgia*, II, 438.

tion and therefore void. The Constitution, he said, gave Congress the power "to provide for organizing, arming, and disciplining the militia, and for governing such part of them as may be employed in the service of the Confederate states, reserving to the states respectively the appointment of the officers." By this clause he understood that Georgia had reserved the right to appoint the officers to command her militia. The Governor contended that by the term "militia" the Constitution meant "the whole arms-bearing population of the state who are not enlisted in the regular army of the Confederacy." In a word, every soldier from Georgia not in the standing army[1] was part of the state militia. The Governor called attention to the opinion of Benjamin that all troops organized and tendered by a state were militia. Furthermore, he contended that the soldiers in the Fifty-first Georgia Regiment, over which the controversy had begun, had enlisted under a promise from the

[1] There had been an attempt to establish a standing army as soon as the Confederacy was organized, but only a few thousand had been thus constituted. Hence, the regular army that Brown referred to was non-existent except in theory, which meant, according to his interpretation, that the Confederate armies were militia, pure and simple.

Secretary that the Governor should commission its officers, and that this promise really amounted to a contract on the part of the Confederate government which it could not violate "without a most unjustifiable breach of its plighted faith."[1]

Seddon explained to Brown that the acts of Congress made a vast distinction between the militia, who were to be officered by the governor, and Confederate troops, whose officers were to be commissioned by the President and Senate. He did not feel, after a careful consideration of the Confederate laws, that he had authority to permit the Governor to appoint officers over Confederate troops, "however agreeable it might be to conform to the wishes of those who have maintained this opinion."[2]

To this argument Brown retorted that he had not called into question the intention of the Confederate law which made a distinction between Confederate troops and state militia and provided that the President should commission the officers. "I think it quite clear," he said, "that it [Congress] intended to confer the appointing power upon the President." However,

[1] O. R., Ser. 4, Vol. II, pp. 620–23.   [2] *Ibid.*, pp. 671–74.

he did question the *right* of Congress to confer this power. It mattered not, he said, what Congress chose to call the arms-bearing population of a state—whether the armies of the Confederacy, or the provisional army, or regular army, or any other name it might choose to adopt—"neither their existence, their identity, nor their character is changed by the name; the arms-bearing population of a state are her militia," and the appointment of their officers a prerogative of the state. He thought that if "by the use of a term or the change of a name" Congress could make militia a part of the Confederate armies, the limit of the usurpation of state rights had been reached. However, as the President had the power, he would have to acquiesce and submit to "a palpable infringement of the rights and sovereignty of the state."[1]

Soon after this the question came up as to who should appoint the officers to command the troops raised for limited service in Georgia. As we will recall, Seddon had called for local-defense companies to be organized under laws of Congress, but the Governor had raised mostly state

[1] O. R., Ser. 4, Vol. II, pp. 737–39; cf. Jones, *Diary*, July 20, 1863.

troops over which he had the undoubted right to appoint officers. Yet he also asserted the right to appoint the officers even over the Confederate units. The Confederate government denied him this right,[1] whereupon he stated that he would commission officers to fill every vacancy reported to him, regardless of the wishes of the war department.[2] General Cobb tried to persuade Brown to desist from such a dangerous course that was bringing the Confederate government and the state into conflict, and which was threatening to "destroy the efficiency of the state-guard service."[3] But the Governor refused to give up the contest, and appealed to the legislature upon the whole question of appointment of officers;[4] and the legislature passed a set of resolutions supporting the position he had taken as to the state's right to officer the troops, and instructed the Georgia representatives in Congress to have the laws altered so as to secure the rights of the state.[5]

[1] O. R., Ser. 1, Vol. LII, Part II, pp. 523–24; *ibid.*, Ser. 4, Vol. II, p. 854.

[2] *Ibid.*, pp. 834–35, 878.   [3] *Ibid.*, p. 878.

[4] *Confederate Records of Georgia*, II, 526–32.

[5] O. R., Ser. 4, Vol. II, pp. 1062–63.

3. THE ATTEMPT OF THE STATES TO SUPPLY THEIR TROOPS IN CONFEDERATE SERVICE

But the most disastrous of all were the efforts of the individual states to furnish supplies for their troops in Confederate service, and the resulting controversies. If the Confederacy had been possessed of large resources, and if it had had unlimited access to foreign supplies, the effect of this individualistic and selfish policy might not have been felt. But as the home resources—such as manufacturing, mining, etc.—and the foreign supplies were very definitely limited, the distribution of supplies, in order to go around, should have been made by a single directing agency with a knowledge of the relative need of each part. Secretary Seddon, who had to contend with the constant attempt of each state to clothe and equip its troops, and who saw better than anyone else the necessity of devolving the duty of supply wholly upon the central government, said:

It is better in every respect that the duty [of supply] should be wholly performed by the Confederate States government, when, in devolving any portion of it upon the states, the means to that extent are withdrawn from the

Confederate government. . . . . If one state undertakes to supply its troops, every other state will be compelled to undertake the same duty. Unequal provision for the soldiers of different states will create jealousy and dissatisfaction among them. . . . . The competitition of the states with each other and the Confederate States would . . . . extend to transportation. . . . . Agencies at home and abroad would be largely multiplied, which would aggravate the competition in every form . . . . whatever is gained by a state is lost by the general service.[1]

President Davis, who was opposed to each state's attempting to supply its troops, expressed a similar view as to its consequences. "If the common supply," he said, "distributed among all is diminished for the purpose of enabling one state to add to the supplies furnished her own ʼtroops, the effect will be pernicious to an extent that can scarcely be appreciated in advance."[2]

The final results of this policy were even worse than was pointed out by either Davis or Seddon. Every state had a swarm of agents competing with Confederate agents, both at home and abroad, causing delay in the already poor

[1] O. R., Ser. 4, Vol. III, pp. 928–29. At this time, though speaking hypothetically, Seddon was actually describing conditions that then existed as a result of the individualistic policy of the states.

[2] *Ibid.*, pp. 948–53.

transportation, increased prices, and ill-will between Confederate and state authorities. The fact that the states did not show sufficient confidence in the Confederate government to allow it to do the common purchasing lowered the confidence of foreign powers in the stability of the government, which in turn hurt its credit. The divided and manifold efforts of the various states to supply the troops multiplied tax and impressment without a corresponding increase in supplies. But above all, this policy resulted in an unequal distribution of supplies among soldiers from states whose resources and facilities for obtaining supplies were unequal, causing jealousy, as Davis and Seddon had pointed out, breaking down the morale, causing wholesale desertions, and a general feeling of bitterness that always results from partiality—though unavoidable—on the part of the government.

It is true that until the Confederate government could organize its supply departments and establish its purchasing machinery, it would be forced to lean upon the states for the clothing and equipment of its troops. So private societies in all the states were organized to make soldiers clothing and equipment,[1] and the states threw in their resources, some arranging to receive the commutation money on condition that they supply the troops. But this was not expected to be a permanent arrangement. The Confederate government planned to take over the whole business as soon as it got "on its feet." However, as has been suggested already, the states did not relinquish their efforts to supply their troops when the Confederacy was ready to take the business over, but really increased them both at home and abroad.

The efforts of the states to supply their troops fall into two distinct fields: the foreign and the domestic. Let us first follow out the policy in the domestic field.

On August 1, 1862, Governor Shorter inquired of Secretary of War Randolph whether the Alabama troops had been sufficiently provided with clothing for the winter. His object, he said, in making the inquiry was "to insure a sufficient supply of clothing to the troops from this state if the state resources" would allow him

[1] *Confederation*, July 19, 1861; *Montgomery Weekly Advertiser*, August 7, 31, 1862.

to do so.[1] On the nineteenth of November following, the legislature passed an act appropriating $250,000 for the purchase of 50,000 pairs of shoes for the Alabama troops, proposing, of course, that the Confederate government should reimburse the state for its expenditures.[2] The war department accepted the arrangement, allowing the state to supply its troops with 50,000 pairs of shoes and a profit of $100,000 in the bargain.[3] Alabama kept up this policy throughout the war, and by 1864 the Governor had evidently got control of the nine factories within the state and was directing their output as best served the interests of Alabama.[4]

Governor Milton, of Florida, was very reluctantly brought into this individualistic policy. He had refused to co-operate with Governor Brown in his efforts to force the Confederate government to allow each state the unlimited right of exportation and importation, and had administered a dignified rebuke to the irrascible

[1] O. R., Ser. 4, Vol. II, p. 32.

[2] *Ibid.*, p. 196; cf. Miller, *History of Alabama*, pp. 157, 167, 168.

[3] O. R., Ser. 4, Vol. II, p. 235.

[4] *Ibid.*, Vol. III, pp. 556–57. Cf. Miller, *History of Alabama*, p. 181.

Brown.[1] He had, it is true, during the early days of the Confederacy, sent his agents into the market to buy private arms and supplies, but as soon as the Confederacy took over the duties of supply he willingly co-operated by withdrawing his separate agents. He saw clearly the short-sightedness of each state's attempting to supply its own troops, yet before the middle of 1864, North Carolina, Georgia, and Alabama having monopolized their resources, compelled him to reverse his policy and insist that the Confederate government relinquish its control of the one factory in Florida.[2]

Georgia went in with a will to supply her troops in Confederate service. Brown, not seeing results fast enough from buying in the open market, recommended in November, 1862, that the legislature seize every factory in Georgia and control the output "till a good pair of shoes and a good suit of clothes are furnished to every [Georgia] soldier in the service who needs the assistance."[3] The assembly approved this meth-

[1] O. R., Ser. 4, Vol. III, pp. 303-4.

[2] *Ibid.*, pp. 499-500, 556-57.

[3] *Confederate Records of Georgia*, II, 266-67.

od,[1] and Brown, either by force or threat, exercised practical control over the factories in Georgia whenever the necessity arose. The expenditures of the state quartermaster department may give us an idea as to the size of this business of supplying troops. In the spring of 1863 Ira J. Foster, state quartermaster, reported to Brown that he had already spent a large portion of the $1,500,000 appropriated in the fall of 1862 for supplying the Georgia soldiers.[2] Three or four months later Brown reported to his legislature that Foster had on hand out of the proceeds of the fund 40,000 uniforms ready for distribution to Georgia troops. A large quantity, he said, had already been distributed. Feeling elated over the success of his quartermaster department, the Governor asked for an appropriation of $2,000,000 to be expended for the same purpose next year,[3] and the legislature granted his request.

Not satisfied with buying all surplus supplies

[1] *Confederate Records of Georgia*, II, pp. 354–55.

[2] *Ibid.*, pp. 408–13.

[3] *Ibid.*, pp. 501–2; *Montgomery Advertiser*, November 11, 1863; January 10, 1864.

in the Georgia market, Brown sent his quarter-master into other states to compete with state and Confederate agents there. He finally got into a row with a district commander in Florida and carried his complaint to the Confederate authorities.[1] General Lawton advised that the separate buying and the separate attempts of the states to supply their own troops was "apt to lead to competition without any material increase of the resources of the country." But he could not stop Brown as there was no legal restriction upon the state agents engaged in the collection of supplies.[2] However, the mere objection to such a policy by the Confederate authorities did not restrain Georgia in her customary habits of clothing her own troops: Governor Brown continued his control over certain of the state's largest factories and, as we shall presently see, redoubled his efforts in blockade-running.

Finally Virginia, whose home resources had been largely under control of the Confederacy, came to the point where the policy of individual state supply seemed necessary. So the Governor, at the instance of S. Bassett French, in the

[1] O. R., Ser. 4, Vol. III, pp. 64-65.   [2] *Ibid.*

summer of 1864, applied to Secretary Seddon for control of the Matoaca factory—the largest in the state.[1] This was the last straw; Quartermaster-General Lawton literally threw up his hands and cried in despair, "et tu, Brute!" He told Seddon that "throughout the extreme southern states one of the greatest difficulties encountered proceeded from the state executives who sought to provide for the wants of the soldiers," and who had consequently monopolized the productions of practically all the factories in their states. "These encroachments and concessions go far," he said, ". . . . to defeat the object in view." He felt satisfied "that it would be better for the state authorities to allow this department to control the factory products so far as they may be needed for military purposes and abstain . . . . from their auxiliary efforts to clothe the army."[2] Now Virginia had asked to control her biggest factory. He was in despair.

However, Virginia seems to have gained control of one of her factories,[3] and later in the year the report of the Governor showed that the state

[1] O. R., Ser. 4, Vol. III, p. 557.

[2] *Ibid.*, pp. 556–58.   [3] *Ibid.*

had gone far on the road pointed out by North
Carolina and Georgia. The Governor informed
the legislature that he had been engaged rather
extensively in the purchase of clothing, cotton,
and other supplies. He was not satisfied, though,
with the matter of transportation: the Confederate government had a prior claim on the trains
in the state, and he thought that Virginia should
assert her rights of priority. This he recommended because in "North Carolina and other
states the practice obtains . . . . that whenever
the governor requires a train on the road for
public use, he issues his orders . . . . and it is
promptly furnished, to the exclusion of all other
demands.[1]

North Carolina alone succeeded in monopolizing the entire output of her factories and getting the lion's share of her other resources during
the entire war. During the period before the
Confederacy had organized and established its
quartermaster department it had quite willingly
made an agreement, in accordance with a resolution of the North Carolina legislature, to pay the
commutation money over to that state and allow

[1] *Ibid.*, pp. 919–20.

it to clothe its own soldiers.[1] But in making this agreement the Confederate government had no intention of withdrawing her agents from North Carolina and turning over all the great manufacturing and natural resources to the exclusive use of that state. Yet that was exactly the manner in which North Carolina interpreted the agreement. North Carolina felt that she had met her every obligation when she supplied her own troops, and accordingly refused to contribute one yard of cloth or a single shoe, or to furnish blankets, tents, harness, and equipment of any kind to the general service during the first year of the war.[2]

This was an unexpected turn of affairs, and the Confederate government attempted to abrogate this misinterpreted agreement in the spring of 1862.[3] But all efforts were in vain. The state only persisted the more in its individualism. The Confederate government next proposed that all clothing and like equipment manufactured in North Carolina should be turned over to the

[1] *Mississippi Valley Historical Review*, December, 1921; O. R., Ser. 4, Vol. II, p. 183; *ibid.*, Vol. III, pp. 671–72, 690–92.

[2] *Ibid.*

[3] *Ibid.*, pp. 690–92; *Mississippi Valley Historical Review*, December, 1921.

Confederate authorities for general issue, on the condition that the troops from that state always be supplied first. But North Carolina refused to budge from her original position.[1]

In October, 1862, the Confederacy finally abolished commutation for clothing and assumed the entire responsibility from thenceforth of clothing the troops in the Confederate service. The Confederate authorities once more attempted to persuade North Carolina to share the output of its factories with the central government, but that state was farther from it than ever,[2] for Vance was now governor and a reactionary legislature had just been elected. The new Governor not only insisted upon monopolizing the entire output of all the factories in the state, but he insisted upon holding the Confederate government to the original agreement, to which he gave the broadest interpretation possible: he insisted that not only the factories but all other resources of North Carolina were also to be entirely devoted to her own use. Now the Confederate government, while unable to obtain any of the

[1] O. R., Ser. 4, Vol. III, pp. 690–92.

[2] *Ibid.; Mississippi Valley Historical Review*, December, 1921.

goods from the factories, had sent agents into North Carolina to pick up whatever they could in the open markets, and Vance, as soon as he assumed office, accused the President and the war department of violating their promises and the agreement that North Carolina should be allowed to devote all her resources to her own troops. He complained that "the country was and still is swarming with agents of the Confederate government, stripping bare our markets and putting enormous prices upon our agents."[1] So until 1864 North Carolina continued her refusal to contribute anything to the general service in the matter of clothing, blankets, shoes, tents, harness, and such equipment.[2] General Lawton, in January, 1864, complained bitterly that North Carolina had forty factories "from not one of which this bureau realized for years past a single yard of material for the service at large. All has been reserved . . . . for North Carolina troops."[3]

[1] O. R., Ser. 4, Vol. II, p. 183; cf. *N.C. Regs.*, I, 25, 26.

[2] *Ibid.*, Vol. III, pp. 690–92; *Mississippi Valley Historical Review*, December, 1921.

[3] O. R., Ser. 4, Vol. III, p. 691.

So great was the need and destitution of the general service by 1864 that the Confederate authorities made a determined effort to obtain a share in the bountiful resources of North Carolina, and only got into a conflict with Vance for their pains. General Lawton spent a good part of his time that year trying to make contracts with the North Carolina factories, but the Governor seemed always to have headed off his attempts before they got results. While Lawton was thus making his futile rounds among the factories, the war department began a wholesale withdrawal of details all over the country. In cases where the details were not withdrawn, they were granted for only a few weeks, thus compelling a constant renewal. Very often details were absolutely refused where before they had been freely granted. This withdrawal of details was not aimed primarily at Vance, and if it had been, as we shall see presently, the shot failed to bring down the game. But Vance was perfectly sure that, like the law suspending the writ of habeas corpus, this measure was meant specially for North Carolina. His factories had been run for the last three years largely by Confederate details whom he had managed to wring out of that sorely beset government, and he was absolutely certain that this withdrawal of details was one of the schemes of the despised Quartermaster-General to get control of his factories. So he sent an indignant protest to Secretary Seddon. General Lawton, he said, had "conceived the idea that the whole business of the state's supplying her own troops must be broken up," and that "accordingly, details for hands in the factories have been refused and . . . . are being sent to camp unless they will break their contracts with the state and enter others with General Lawton." Such a disregard for North Carolina's rights by a Confederate agent, he said, "will not be submitted to."[1]

The Confederate government, in spite of the protest of Vance, continued to withdraw details. On October 5 and 8, 1864, Confederate General Orders Nos. 76 and 77 restricted details to a very narrow limit. But Governor Vance was determined to have all the men he needed if he had to withdraw the North Carolina troops from Vir-

[1] O. R., Ser. 4, Vol. III, pp. 671–72; cf. Jones, *Diary*, I, 290. Lawton really had nothing to do with the withdrawal of details (*ibid.*, pp. 690–92).

ginia to accomplish his purpose. He sent a list of the men he wished continued on detail in his factories to General Holmes, who was commander of the department. He warned the general that "should these details . . . . be unreasonably refused, I shall have to try tilts with the Confederate government."[1] Failing to obtain all he asked for, Vance placed himself upon higher ground: he claimed "any and all persons in the actual employ of the state" as state officers, and thus obtained the exemption of his factory operatives, where before he had only had them detailed. The state legislature, by a set of resolutions, indorsed this position, and the supreme court of the state upheld it in the case of Johnson *vs.* Mallet. So the wheels of the North Carolina mills turned on unvexed by dependence upon Confederate detail, and North Carolina went through the war without making any contributions from her output to the general service.[2]

More than that, North Carolina drew largely from other states. The state purchased the much-needed wool from Virginia right under the very nose of the Confederate government; it

[1] *Ibid.*, p. 746.   [2] *Ibid.*, pp. 754-55.

bought up quantities of leather in Georgia and Florida, and even procured war material in large quantities from the trans-Mississippi department, thus still further diminishing the already meager sources for Confederate supplies.[1] As a result of this and her blockade policy, North Carolina had on hand, while the Confederate soldiers from other states were freezing and dying from exposure, large stores of clothing and blankets. In December, 1863, North Carolina had all her troops warmly clad and had on hand —stored at Richmond, Raleigh, and other points —a surplus sufficient to meet the needs of the troops for the entire year of 1864 if the mills had not put out another yard.[2] General Gardiner reported a vast quantity of North Carolina clothing stored in Richmond in the summer of 1864. This clothing had been there for over a year.[3] At the time of the surrender Vance had, according to his own count, 92,000 uniforms, great stores of leather and blankets, and his troops in the field were all comfortably clad.[4] At the same

[1] O. R., Ser. 4, Vol. III, pp. 690-92.
[2] Ibid., pp. 690-91.   [3] Ibid., p. 691.
[4] Southern Historical Society Papers, XIV, 513; cf. N.C. Regs., I, 34-35. Part of these stores of supplies were blockade goods. See pp. 127-49.

time Lee's troops were ragged and without blankets and tents.

Thus most of the Confederate states had adopted the individualistic policy of supplying their own troops, some withdrawing a part and some all of their industrial resources from the Confederate government. The consideration of a few statistics of southern resources will enable us to understand the result better. There were only 122 mills within the Confederacy in 1864. There were 9 in Alabama, 9 in South Carolina, 1 in Florida, 1 in Mississippi, 26 in Virginia, 36 in Georgia (5 of which had been wrecked), and 40 in North Carolina (well equipped and large). Out of this total of 122 mills, the states of Virgiania, Georgia, Alabama, North Carolina, and Florida were controlling 54, while the Confederate government controlled only 68, part of which were later destroyed or fell into the hands of the enemy.[1]

The products of the foreign markets were still more unevenly distributed than the output of the home industries, and a smaller percentage was directed toward the common service. The

[1] O. R., Ser. 4, Vol. III, pp. 690–92; cf. *ibid.*, pp. 556–58.

seaboard states had agents in the foreign markets floating loans and purchasing and shipping supplies from the first. As early as August, 1861, we hear of Georgia's representative, E. C. Anderson, making a purchase of $100,000 worth of supplies.[1] North Carolina in 1861 sent John L. Payton as a special agent to purchase supplies,[2] and in the fall of 1862 it sent John White and T. M. Crosson as regular commissioners,[3] and Virginia, South Carolina, Alabama, and Texas evidently had their representatives.[4] These states, after the first year and a half of the war had usually one or two vessels with which to import and export through the blockade, and for the rest they would have to depend upon the professional blockade runners with whom they entered contracts or in which they bought shares.

The Confederate government had only three or four small vessels of its own with which to run the blockade.[5] These could only bring in a small

[1] O. R., Ser. 4, Vol. I, p. 559.   [2] Ibid., p. 692.

[3] Ibid., Vol. II, pp. 194-95.

[4] *Annual Cyclopaedia* (1863), pp. 8, 829; and Jones, *Diary*, I, 222.

[5] Schwab, *Confederate States*, p. 254; O. R., Ser. 4, Vol. III, p. 553. Right at the end of the war the Confederate states were beginning a program of extensive government ownership.

fraction of the materials purchased abroad by the government, and like the states, it too was dependent upon the professional blockade-runners for the greater part of its import and export trade. Thus we see that both the Confederate and state governments were largely dependent upon the private blockade-runners for the exportation and importation of their supplies. The result was a cutthroat competition to obtain control of the blockade vessels, and the corporations that owned these ships took advantage of the necessity of the Confederacy and exacted enormous profits. They brought goods into the Confederate ports for which they were allowed unreasonable prices, and received in payment Confederate cotton at the rate of six cents a pound, which they sold in Europe at twenty-four pence. President Davis pointed out, in a message to Congress, that six hundred bales delivered to these blockade-runners netted the Confederate states only £6,000, while it brought the shipowners £21,000, allowing a liberal estimate of 11 per cent loss by capture.[1] In addition

[1] *Ibid.*, p. 952; see also *ibid.*, pp. 529–30, 553, 588, 954–55; Jones, *Diary*, I, 239; see also Freemantle, *Three Months in the Southern States*, pp. 132, 133, 202–3, for description of blockade-runners.

to this the profit on the imported goods was just as great. The efforts of the states to make contracts with these vessels were partly responsible for these prices.

This was the situation until the middle of 1863, when the Confederate government attempted to extricate itself by hitting upon the idea of renting one-third of the space on each vessel, which it proposed to use to import and export supplies and cotton on its own responsibility.[1] The states again entered upon a competitive race and forced the rental of the space obtained on these vessels to the most unreasonable level.[2] Due, however, to heavy pressure upon these shipowners, the Confederate government was at length, in the fall of 1863, in spite of the state competition, enabled to make a contract for one-third space on all their boats.[3] But these contracts proved very onerous to the states, which wanted to ship out their cotton and import supplies for their own troops, and to the steamship companies, who saw further opportunity to exact higher toll. So the shipowners

[1] O. R., Ser. 4, Vol. III, pp. 28, 554; and Jones, *Diary*, II, 14.
[2] O. R., Ser. 4, Vol. III, p. 554.   [3] *Ibid.*, pp. 28, 554.

and the seaboard states drew together in their common affliction and formed a combine that proposed to leave the Confederacy entirely out of the shipping business. Each of these states purchased a share in the various steamers or chartered them outright—with the evident understanding that the chartered vessels would continue to carry a large part of the cargoes on the private account of the companies while enjoying the protection of a state charter. South Carolina and Georgia purchased shares in the Importing and Exporting Company of South Carolina[1]—perhaps the largest concern in the Confederacy. North Carolina bought shares in the steamers of Collie and Company,[2] and Virginia seems to have adopted a similar course.[3]

This pre-emption of blockade-runners for the moment cut off all means, except its own four vessels, which the Confederacy had of exporting its cotton and importing cloth and arms, etc. It was once more thrown upon the mercy of the blockade-runner, who had been aiming all along at forcing the Confederacy entirely out of busi-

[1] *Ibid.*, Vol. II, p. 1060; Schwab, *Confederate States*, p. 257.

[2] *Ibid.*, Vol. III, pp. 10–11.   [3] *Ibid.*, pp. 114, 161–62.

ness. But it refused to submit without a struggle to this unscrupulous arrangement: it insisted upon holding these ships to their contracts to carry one-third of their cargo on Confederate account. Naturally, in doing so it ran afoul of the seaboard states and became involved in several controversies from which it finally came out second-best.

South Carolina became very much concerned when the Confederate government attempted to force the unscrupulous shipowners of the Importing and Exporting Company and the Bee Line, in which she was interested, to carry out their contracts. In December, 1863, the legislature passed resolutions instructing the Governor to do all in his power to cause the Confederate government to relinquish the rights heretofore claimed of shipping cotton and bringing freight on the ships owned by the above-named companies "in consequence of the ownership of that state of a part of these boats," in order that South Carolina might import supplies for her troops.[1]

Governor Bonham placed the matter before

[1] O. R., Ser. 4, Vol. II, p. 1060.

the war department, which had in its charge
most of the business of foreign supplies at this
time. But Seddon made no response for several
weeks, due to the fact that he was waiting for
Congress to pass the bill then before it that
would regulate the whole question of import and
export.[1] On January 27, 1864, the Governor became so worried over having had no response to
his proposition to the war department that he
sent a personal representative, Charles M. Furman, for a conference with the Secretary of War.[2]
The Secretary had to give some kind of answer,
for he was at last cornered by Mr. Furman and
A. P. Aldrich, who also represented the Governor. He finally agreed to allow South Carolina
to pre-empt the use of the ships until the bill
regulating the question should become a law.[3] A
similar situation came up in the case of Virginia,
and the temporary pre-emption of the vessels in
question was also allowed that state.[4]

In North Carolina the Confederate government stirred up a hornet's nest when it attempted to enforce its contracts with the steamship

[1] *Ibid.*, Vol. III, pp. 77-78.   [3] *Ibid.*, pp. 77-78; 161-62.

[2] *Ibid.*, p. 51.   [4] *Ibid.*, pp. 161-62.

companies. Governor Vance flatly refused to allow any of the steamers in which North Carolina had acquired a share to put on board a bale of Confederate cotton.[1] Two days after this, January 6, 1864, Seddon remonstrated against the Governor's obstructiveness, telling him that "the necessities of the government really require adherence to this regulation," and that he hoped he would not encourage or allow the infringement of the contract requiring the shipowners to carry one-third on government account.[2] The next day the Governor replied that North Carolina had 40,000 blankets, 40,000 pairs of shoes, large quantities of clothing, leather, and other supplies at Bermuda, and that he must have all the steamers in which North Carolina had an interest to carry these goods. Vance finally worked himself into a rage over the thought that the Confederate government had interfered with his efforts to monopolize the home resources of North Carolina for the troops from that state, and that now it was attempting to interfere with his import and export trade which was being carried on largely to supply his troops. "It is a

[1] O. R., Ser. 4, Vol. III, p. 4.   [2] *Ibid.*

little remarkable . . . . ," he said, "that the entire importing operations of this state, which have been so successful . . . . seem to have met with little else than downright opposition rather than encouragement from the Confederate government.[1] In its very inception Mr. Mason, our commissioner in England, laid the strong hands on my agents and positively forbade them putting a bond on the market for five months after they landed in England." Then came the delays of his ships at Wilmington, and the impressment of his coal by the Confederate government to furnish the privateers. Now, he said, the climax had been reached in the attempt of the government to force private blockade-runners in which

[1] North Carolina had entered the importing business in the latter part of 1862. Adjutant General Martin suggested the purchase of a ship and Governor Vance adopted the idea. The "Ad-Vance" was purchased and blockade-running got to be a paying business. The "Ad-Vance" soon paid for itself and brought millions of dollars' worth of supplies and carried out cotton to pay for them. Within a year Governor Vance reported to his legislature that he had enough supplies, with those obtainable at home, to supply his troops till 1865 if he did not get another dollar's worth from abroad (*North Carolina Regiments*, I, 16–19, 20, 30–34, 35). Business increased steadily till the fall of Wilmington. Major Gordon says this business endeared Vance to the people of the state "more than any other act of his life, perhaps more than all others combined" (*ibid.*, pp. 16–19.)

North Carolina had an interest to carry a third of their cargoes on government account. He felt sure that the companies would stop all their vessels, since there would be no profit left, and as to the ones in which North Carolina was interested, if the regulations were enforced he would countermand their sailing.[1]

On January 14 Seddon replied that the steamship companies whom Vance had taken under his special protection were all foreigners, solely interested in getting as much cotton as possible on their own account out of the country in return for as little service and sacrifice as possible, and that in pursuance of this object they were taking the states, who exacted only one-fourth of their cargo, into a partnership in order to avoid their contracts with the Confederacy, which exacted one-third of their cargo. Besides, if the states should acquire as much cargo space as the Confederate government, it would be unwise for them to do so, for, he said, it would be better "for the Confederate government to send out cotton to procure supplies for our armies than for the individual states to un-

[1] O. R., Ser. 4, Vol. III, pp. 10–11.

dertake the matter. Some states have no port; others are within the occupation of the enemy. . . . . If each state undertakes the export and import of all supplies necessary, we shall have great jealousy among the troops from the different states, and great embarrassment in questions connected with transportation." However, as in the case of Virginia and South Carolina, Seddon was compelled to allow the temporary exemption from Confederate contracts of all steamers owned in part by North Carolina.[1]

Soon afterward, on February 7, 1864, the law upon which Seddon had been basing his expectations passed. It empowered the President to draw up a uniform set of regulations to cover all private import and export trade, leaving the states free to carry on their own trade in vessels owned entirely by the state. Immediately the President made the rule that all ships going out and coming in must carry one-half of their cargoes on Confederate account.[2] This was aimed directly at such concerns as the South Carolina Importing and Exporting Company, the Bee

[1] *Ibid.*, pp. 28–29.

[2] *Ibid.*, pp. 80–82, 113–14, 187–89.

Line, and Collie and Company, who had transferred part of their interests to the several states
in order to dodge their contracts with the Confederate government; and it meant prolonged
and bitter opposition. The states made the fight
their own. They invited the steamship companies into some very questionable arrangements
in order that they might avoid the regulations
requiring that one-half of their cargo be on Confederate account. One of these, and apparently
the one most universally made, was the entire
transfer of all the private ships by charter to the
individual states. This, it was hoped, would
place these ships upon the same basis as those
entirely owned by the state governments, which,
as we have seen, were exempt from the Confederate regulations.[1] If the Confederate government
had permitted this flagrant violation of the spirit
of the law, it would have been left permanently
at the mercy and whim of the blockade-runners
in its efforts to obtain foreign supplies and export
its cotton. But the President and the Secretary
of War refused to allow clearance papers to any

[1] O. R., Ser. 1, Vol. LI, Part II, p. 841; *ibid.*, Ser. 4, Vol. IV, pp.
552-55.

ship not actually owned by a state, unless the ship complied with the Confederate regulations.

Governor Vance, who was the leader in this scheme to oust the Confederacy from the import and export trade, proposed to Seddon that North Carolina would buy one-third interest in the ships in which North Carolina already had a small share, on condition that the Confederate government would release said ships from the regulations.[1] But the Secretary of War refused to entertain such a proposition, explaining that the regulations made no exceptions to any ships save those entirely owned by the state. Vance was already engaged in a nasty personal controversy with President Davis over the suspense of the writ of habeas corpus, impressment, and peace proposals,[2] so this refusal to allow him the pre-emption of such private vessels as he wanted by the purchase of a third interest was more than he could endure. On March 5 he wired Seddon: "Is it possible that such an unblushing outrage is intended by the government? I have no com-

[1] *Ibid.*, Vol. III, pp. 153-54.

[2] See chapter on habeas corpus, impressment, also O. R., Ser. 1, Vol. LI, Part II, pp. 807, 808, 814, 818, 824, 830, 837, 841, 844.

ment to make on such proceedings further than that I will fire the ships before I will agree to it."[1]

Governor Brown chartered the "Little Ada," "Florrie," "Little Hattie," "Lillian," and another from the Importing and Exporting Company of Georgia in order to block the Confederate program[2] and carry on his own export trade. On April 9 the Governor wired the Secretary of the Treasury to give clearance papers for the steamer, "Little Ada," which was loaded heavily with cotton, but not a bale of which was on Confederate account. This was an open violation of the regulations, so the Secretary refused him the papers.[3] Joe Brown, who, like Vance, was at the moment engaged in a struggle with the Confederate government over the same questions, became highly indignant. He immediately called upon the several governors of the states east of the Mississippi to join him in a conference in which plans might be formulated to cause a repeal or different interpretation of the Confederate law. Governors Watts, Clark, and

[1] O. R., Ser. 1, Vol. LI, Part II, pp. 828–29.
[2] *Confederate Records of Georgia*, II, 581, 752–58.
[3] O. R., Ser. 4, Vol. III, p. 416.

Vance readily consented to join in this indignation meeting, but Governors Smith and Milton refused.[1]

A few days after this, on April 18, Governors Clark of Mississippi, Vance of North Carolina, Watts of Alabama, and Brown of Georgia drew up a protest against the Confederate regulations of trade. They insisted that Davis had misinterpreted the law and had overstepped his rightful authority in drafting these regulations, for the law plainly said that nothing in its provisions was to be construed as restraining the state in its right to export on its own responsibility, and that was, they protested, just what the President had done. However, they added, if the President had given the proper interpretation to the law, they would demand that Congress instantly re-

[1] *Ibid.*, pp. 303–4. Governor Milton, in reply to Brown's invitation to participate in the proposed meeting, administered the Governor of Georgia a dignified rebuke for his proposed attempts to influence Congress to repeal the law, and for the short-sighted and injurious policy of each state's attempting to clothe and equip its own troops. He pointed out the same evil results of the "attempt on the part of the states separately to relieve the necessities of the armies," as Seddon and Davis had done. The final result of the whole policy, he said, would be to cause the armies of the Confederacy to suffer and "endanger the stability of the Confederate government, if not entirely destroy it by a separation of states."

peal the law, for it was a dangerous infringement of state rights. They "could not yield their assent to the doctrine that the Confederate States government has any right to impose any such restrictions upon the states." This group of state-rights governors also left a perfectly unmistakable record of their attitude toward the matter of supplying the troops, especially from foreign sources. While they realized the importance of import and export to the Confederacy, they said, yet they were of the opinion that it was far "better that each state government should conduct its own business for itself" and every state "provide for the comfort of its own troops."[1] The governors had been acting upon this principle already, but this is the first instance of its formulation in such bald terms. State sovereignty could go little farther.

Having obtained the solid backing of the state-rights governors, and having started an agitation in the Confederate Congress for the repeal of the obnoxious trade-regulations law, Brown returned to pick up his quarrel with the

[1] Moore, *Rebellion Record*, VIII, 596–97; cf. *Confederate Records of Georgia*, II, 752–58.

Confederate government over the "Little Ada."
On April 27 application was made again for
clearance papers, and again refused unless Brown
would agree to load one-half of the "Little
Ada's" cargo with Confederate cotton.[1] The
Confederate government would be willing to give
clearance for any ship owned by the state of
Georgia, but this vessel was a private blockade-
runner in which the state probably had purchased a small share. On May 9 Brown again
wired Davis for a clearance, and once more the
Confederate authorities explained that the "Little Ada" must carry half a cargo on the Confederacy's account.[2] On May 21 the Governor
replied to Secretary Memminger, whom he had
dragged into the controversy, that he denied the
right of any executive officer to repeal "by his
order" the act which conceded each state the
right to export on its own account. "I therefore
demand," he said, "clearance as a right, not as
a favor."[3] On May 23 Memminger gave his final
refusal to allow the "Little Ada" clearance pa-

[1] *Rebellion Record*, VIII, 596–97; O. R., Ser. 4, Vol. III, p. 416.
[2] *Ibid.*
[3] *Ibid.*, p. 439; *Rebellion Record*, VIII, 596–97.

pers.[1] Sometime after this, Brown protested to his legislature that Davis's interference with state blockade-running "was a palpable assumption of power and an utter disregard of every principle of state's rights and state sovereignty."[2]

In the meanwhile, the seaboard states had not confined their opposition to attempting to get control over private vessels by "charter" or to governors' meetings and controversy: they had engineered the entire blockade-runner fleet into going out on a strike of several weeks.[3] This was a very hurtful move against the Confederacy, as the much-needed imports and exports were cut off at a critical period;[4] but it was considered a legitimate weapon to use in bringing the refractory central government to terms.

To this campaign against the Confederate law regulating trade was now added the weight of the state-rights party in Congress. The Sec-

[1] O. R., Ser. 4, Vol. III, p. 442; *Rebellion Record*, VIII, 596–97.

[2] *Confederate Records of Georgia*, II, 752–58.

[3] O. R., Ser. 4, Vol. III, pp. 948–53; cf. *ibid.*, pp. 953–58.

[4] About the beginning of Grant's Virginia campaign against Lee, and Sherman's against Johnston. Lee's men were ragged and without tents and blankets, and this strike contributed to this condition.

ond Confederate Congress, fresh from the election broils in which anti-Davis and anti-war propaganda had been widespread, contained a large number who were willing to dissolve the Confederacy and allow each state to assume its complete sovereignty, set up for itself, or enter negotiations for a separate peace with the Union. This group welcomed the protest of the governors' meeting, which had been placed in their hands, as a bone of contention. In accordance with the tone of the governors' protest against Confederate interference with state export, Mr. Hartridge, of Georgia, on March 3, 1864, introduced a resolution in the House inquiring "whether .... the secretary of the treasury has the right to prevent the sailing of vessels owned or chartered by any of the states" because these vessels had refused to obey the Confederate regulations.[1] Congress pushed the question right on through both houses and passed a bill that would leave no room for doubt, as the first one had. All ships that were owned in part or "chartered" to the state by these steamship companies were to be exempted from

[1] *Journal of the Confederate Congress*, VII, 13.

the Confederate regulations.[1] The President, who had a knowledge of all the facts in the case, vetoed this bill on June 10. He pointed out that if the ships chartered by the states were exempted from the regulations it would be at the grave risk of the Confederacy's being "deprived of this indispensable means of carrying on the war," because all owners already had either chartered their ships to the state or had "threatened to transfer their vessels to the executives of the several states and thus withdraw them from the operation of the regulations." He pointed out how great had been the results of the regulations so far in strengthening Confederate credit abroad and enabling it to pay up its debts. To repeal the law and enact the proposed bill would be calamitous.[2] Not satisfied with the veto of this bill, the Congress passed an amendment in the last hours of the session which proposed to exempt all vessels already chartered at the time from the Confederate regulations, and again President Davis was forced to withhold his approval for the same

[1] O. R., Ser. 4, Vol. III, pp. 552–55.

[2] *Journal of the Confederate Congress*, VII, 206; IV, 209; O. R., Ser. 4, Vol. III, pp. 553–55.

reasons as he had set forth in his veto message of the previous bill on the same subject. He had been credibly informed that practically every ship in the blockade service had been chartered to the state executives in anticipation of this law.[1]

Congress, immediately after convening in the fall of 1864, took up the agitation of the matter again. On December 5 the Senate passed a resolution that the President be requested to inform the Senate "whether any and what restrictions had been imposed upon the exercise of the right of the Confederate states or any of them to export on their own account," and whether the law ought to be repealed or modified.[2] The next day the House passed similar resolutions;[3] and on December 20, Davis replied. He again pointed out, as in his veto, the danger of exempting private vessels or vessels "chartered" to the states. He showed how greatly the law had aided the Confederate finances. Because of its ability to

[1] O. R., Ser. 4, Vol. III, pp. 552-53.

[2] *Journal of Confederate Congress*, IV, 313; O. R., Ser. 4, Vol. III, p. 897.

[3] *Ibid.*, p. 897.

ship cotton on its own account the Confederacy was realizing the handsome price of $200 a bale, whereas under the contract systems, where the blockade-runners had contracted to bring goods in exchange for Confederate cotton to be delivered at port, it had realized only $50, and that the goods could be obtained far cheaper by direct purchase in Europe than by purchase from the blockade-runners.[1] The cry that the law was ruining private enterprise, he said, was all propaganda to force a repeal of the law. This was clearly shown from the fact that the number of vessels taking part in the trade had rapidly increased during 1864 in spite of the growing stringency of the blockade, and that the stock in one of these companies, originally selling for $2,000 a share, was in July, 1864, selling at $20,000 a share.[2]

[1] The system of government regulation was bringing in magnificent returns in spite of all opposition. Within three months, from October 1, 1864, to January 2, 1865, 500,000 pairs of shoes, 800,000 pounds of bacon, 2,000,000 pounds of saltpeter, 316,000 pairs of blankets, 69,000 rifles, and other supplies had been brought through the blockade. One can readily see what would have been the results if the Confederate states had been able to regulate this traffic from the first and had had the co-operation of the states. See Jones, *Diary*, II, 262, 373, 375; also Rhodes, Vol. V.

[2] O. R., Ser. 4, Vol. III, pp. 928, 948–58; *Journal of the Confederate Congress*, IV, 373–76.

But Congress, nothing more by this time than a delegation of ambassadors from the "sovereign states," gave no heed to the President's warnings. On March 4 and 8, 1865, the two houses passed a bill that removed all restrictions and left the Confederacy stripped bare of all its means of exportation and importation.[1]

Thus in their efforts to obtain a share in the export and import business of the country, the states had by their own vessels withdrawn large quantities of supplies from the common agent, and they had by charters and purchases of shares in private vessels often driven the Confederacy practically out of the import business; by fomenting strikes among the shipping companies they had suspended the blockade-running entirely for several weeks, and by their factiousness added immeasurably to the already deep discontent of the masses of people.[2]

[1] *Journal of the Confederate Congress*, VII, 694, 720.

[2] For accounts of blockade-running see Taylor, *Running the Blockade*; Watson, *Adventures of a Blockade-Runner*; Soley, *Blockade and the Cruisers*; Wilkinson, *Narrative of a Blockade-Runner*; Scharf, *Confederate Navy*; Fleming, *Civil War and Reconstruction in Alabama*, pp. 183–88; Rhodes, Vol. V; Schwab, *History of the Confederacy*, pp. 251–66.

CHAPTER III

THE SUSPENSION OF THE WRIT OF HABEAS CORPUS

The controversies over local defense and the attempts of the states in part to control their troops in Confederate service were soon paralleled by bitter quarrels between the states and the central government over the suspension of the writ of habeas corpus. The latter controversies were waged about the three laws passed during the second and fourth years of the Confederacy: (*a*) that of February 27, 1862 (and its amendment, April 19); (*b*) that of October 13, 1862, which expired February 13, 1863; and (*c*) the law of February 15, 1864, which expired August 1, 1864.

I. FIRST LAW AND AMENDMENT, FEBRUARY 27 AND APRIL 19, 1862, EXPIRING OCTOBER 13, 1862

In the spring of 1862 the Confederacy seemed to be going to pieces—army desertion, capture of Fort Donelson and New Orleans—and among the strong measures taken to pull the disintegrating structure together was the law of February 27, suspending the writ of habeas corpus under certain conditions. The law granted the President authority during the invasion to suspend the privilege of the writ and to declare martial law in those cities, towns, and districts threatened by the enemy.[1] This was a grant of vast powers to the President, but unlike Lincoln, he made a very limited use of them and proceeded cautiously—one might say hesitatingly—considering the fact that Davis was a bold and courageous man and that the needs in the spring of 1862 were so great. The reason for such moderation was the extreme sensitiveness of the southern states to any appearance of centralizing tendencies or of Confederate encroachment upon the reserved rights of the states. Instead of proclaiming martial law and suspending the writ of habeas corpus in all the border states and along the long lines of seacoast, he singled out only those points that were in the most imminent danger from the enemy. He placed Nor-

[1] O. R., Ser. 4, Vol. I, p. 954; Schwab, *Confederate States*, p. 186.

folk, Portsmouth, and the immediately sur-
rounding country under martial law as soon as
the law was passed, but showed his desire not
to shock the sensibilities of the people by sug-
gesting that the mayor of Norfolk be appointed
provost marshal for that city.[1] Bearing out this
policy, the civil and military governor of the
city issued a proclamation stating that, subject
to the judgment of the general of the department,
the ordinances and laws of the city would govern
his action in its administration in cases of contract and misdemeanor.[2] On March 8 martial
law was extended over Petersburg and the sur-
rounding country, but the courts were left to
function under supervision in certain cases such
as probating wills, granting divorces, alimony,
and injunctions, appointing guardians, and de-
termining the custody of children, etc.[3] Richmond was placed under martial law, with only
the mayor left to perform his civil function.[4]
Mobile and New Orleans, with the neighboring

[1] O. R., Ser. 1, Vol. IX, pp. 46, 56.

[2] *Ibid.*, Vol. LI, Part II, pp. 490–91.

[3] *Ibid.*, p. 493.

[4] *Ibid.*, p. 482; Stephenson, *Day of the Confederacy*, pp. 41–42;
Rhodes, III, 603; Schwab, p. 186.

counties, were placed under martial law about the middle of March, 1862.[1]

But because of disapproval on the part of the people, whom Davis was careful to consider as far as possible in this matter, he did not suspend the writ, under the law of February 27, in any part of Georgia, North Carolina, South Carolina, Tennessee, Texas, and Arkansas.

Yet in spite of this conservative, sparing use of the power granted him by the first law, Davis's course aroused suspicion and hostility immediately. This was especially true in Richmond and New Orleans. General Winder was made military governor of the former city and he cleaned out the city from center to circumference. Spies, traitors, loafers, slackers, all were swept out, saloons and gambling dens closed—in short, order was brought out of chaos. Winder was not overgentle in his methods: he employed two hundred spies and deputies to pick up rumor and gossip, and consequently made arrests in high circles. The result was that he aroused bitter opposition to martial law and brought down upon the administration the con-

[1] O. R., Ser. 1, Vol. LII, Part II, pp. 290–91; *ibid.*, Vol. VI, 856, 866.

demnation of a powerful group of men among whom was the newspaper editor, Pollard.[1]

In New Orleans, which was practically in a state of anarchy, General Lovell had issued an order that all over sixteen would be required to take an oath of allegiance or get out, and that every person must carry a passport signed by the provost marshal.[2] This, with other objectionable features of martial law, was more than the Louisiana governor could tolerate without protest. Lovell had once before attempted to establish order and restore the morale of the people by declaring martial law on his own responsibility, and the Governor evidently preferred chaos to a second experience. "It would not be expected," he wrote Davis, "that I would ever again consent to the proclamation of mar-

[1] Stephenson, *Day of the Confederacy*, pp. 41–42; Rhodes, III, 603. There seems to be little doubt that Winder played the part of the despot under this as well as later laws. His personality was unfortunate, and to add further to his unpopularity he brought over his "plug ugly" gang of detectives from Maryland who were, according to Jones, a bunch of "roughnecks," blackmailers, and too often traitors or spies. One gets the impression from his diary that Winder alienated more friends from Davis than any other cause. See Jones, *Diary*, I, 115, 116, 120, 121, 150, 154, 159, 178, 293, as illustrations.

[2] O. R., Ser. 1, Vol. VI, pp. 857–58.

tial law by General Lovell after the urgent and persistent complaints I made to you of the action of his provost marshals which received his silent acquiescence if not his open approval.[1]"

The Confederate Congress became alarmed at the possibilities of martial law as experienced in Richmond,[2] so they immediately passed an amendment to the law of February 27 that cut down the authority of the President as well as limited the duration of the law. The amendment became a law on April 19, less than two months after the passage of the first law, and it provided that the power to suspend the writ should be limited to arrests made by the Confederate government and to offenses against its laws, and that it should continue in force not more than thirty days after the next meeting of Congress. Furthermore, the power to declare martial law was not mentioned in the new law.[3] Undoubtedly Congress intended by this law to prevent a repetition of such an occurrence as that of Richmond and New Orleans. Apparently, the

[1] *Ibid.*, Vol. XV, p. 740.

[2] See Jones, *Diary*, I, 115, 116, 120.

[3] O. R., Ser. 4, Vol. I, p. 1075; Schwab, p. 186.

law meant to withhold the right of interfering with the operation of state courts and authorities, and of superseding civil with military government. It meant that the writ could not be withheld except in case of offense against the Confederate laws.

But there was apparently no clear distinction in the minds of most of the Confederate officers between the original and the amended law. This was due, probably, to the vague and general meanings attached to the terms "martial law" and the "suspension of the writ of habeas corpus." Most of the military leaders and Confederate authorities considered the two terms as identical in meaning, or at least one term was supposed to include the other in its meaning. They held the opinion that the power to establish martial law inhered in the power to suspend the writ. Hence, though the law of April 19 granted only the power to suspend the writ, it was assumed without any question that it carried the power to declare martial law. The result was that not only was the writ continued suspended in the former districts, but it was suspended in portions of all the other southern states under the second law, and martial law was established with the attendant suspension of the civil jurisdiction.

Davis suspended the writ in Salisbury, North Carolina, June 5, 1862,[1] and on May 1 he proclaimed martial law in South Carolina from the Santee River to the South Edisto River, including Charleston.[2] But the most sweeping extensions of martial law—and the most alarming—in the summer of 1862 were made by four military commanders. There had been some thought of establishing martial law in Augusta and Savannah as well as other parts of Georgia,[3] but because of opposition from Savannah, Davis had not pushed the matter. General Bragg, however, took matters into his own hands, and on August 11, 1862, placed Atlanta under martial law.[4]

On May 30 General P. O. Hèbert established martial law over the entire state of Texas, without consulting the President. Every white per-

[1] O. R., Ser. 2, Vol. III, p. 890; *ibid.*, Ser. 1, Vol. XVIII, p. 793.

[2] *Ibid.*, Vol. XIV, pp. 489, 491–92, 570–71.

[3] *Ibid.*, pp. 478–79.

[4] O. R., Ser. 1, Vol. XVI, Part II, p. 754.

son above the age of sixteen within the state limits must register his age, name, address, and occupation with a provost marshal, and answer such questions and impart such information as might be required of him; all persons failing to meet the required terms or all persons suspected of disloyalty were to leave the state immediately; all orders of the provost marshals in the execution of their duty must be promptly obeyed —anyone failing to do so was subject to summary punishment; and the civil authorities, while they were to continue their function, were placed under supervision of the military authorities.[1]

In the spring of 1862 Arkansas was virtually without any kind of government, for after the withdrawal of Van Dorn a general stampede had followed and nearly all civil authority had abdicated. Guerilla and partisan warfare, bushwhacking, and pillaging were on every side. There was security for neither person nor property. Furthermore, the country, as a result of the attitude of Governor Rector toward the Confederate government, had become a haven of

[1] O. R., Ser. 1, Vol. IX, p. 716.

refuge for thousands of Arkansas and Texas troops deserting from the east side of the Mississippi River. Something had to be done, so General Hindman, who had assumed temporary command in the Arkansas country, took all responsibility upon his own shoulders and proclaimed martial law June 30, 1862, placing a provost martial in every neighborhood with a detail of soldiers to back him, and put Arkansas in order and to a great extent restored the morale of the people.[1]

In Mississippi and East Louisiana, during the spring and summer of 1862, conditions were as bad as they were in Arkansas before Hindman assumed command. Furthermore, Federal armies were marching to and fro over that region trying to bag the Confederate troops, and now, if ever in their existence, a strong government was needed in these two states to prevent the complete demoralization of the people and to safeguard the armies from spies, bridge-burners, and defection. General Van Dorn, who commanded parts of this district, did as Hèbert, Bragg, and Hindman had done, assumed the

[1] *Ibid.*, Vol. XIII, pp. 38, 40, 44, 835-36.

responsibility of dealing with the situation according to his own judgment. So on July 4, 1862, he proclaimed martial law over all Louisiana east of the Mississippi River, and over the Mississippi counties of Issaquena, Yazoo, Warren, Hinds, Holmes, Claiborne, Hancock, Harrison, Jackson, Carroll, and Sunflower. Van Dorn had a clear idea as to what martial law meant; and in his proclamation, though he disclaims any purpose of interfering more than was necessary with civil or criminal courts, he reminded the people that martial law "has been well defined to be the will of the military commander." He laid down some exceedingly severe regulations. Anyone who traded with the enemy—an everyday occurrence in that country—or attempted to pass the enemy's lines or give information to the enemy should suffer death. Any person who refused to accept Confederate money—another common thing in a district so near the enemy's lines—or said or did anything to depreciate Confederate currency should be fined and imprisoned. Finally, and most dangerous of all, his proclamation threatened the freedom of speech and the press. In part, it said:

> The publication of any article in the newspapers in reference to the movements of troops is prohibited, and if the editor or proprietor of any newspaper publishes in any editorial or copies into his paper any article or paragraph calculated to impair confidence in any of the commanding officers . . . . such editor or proprietor shall be subject to fine and imprisonment and the publication of the paper shall be thereafter suspended.[1]

Naturally there was protest, bitter and prolonged, against both authorized and unauthorized establishment of martial law. Even the friends of the administration and the champions of the law suspending the writ had difficulty proving that it did not clearly violate the most sacred of state rights, while the enemies of the administration and of martial law saw in the power exercised by the President and his generals an indication that Davis and the army were bent upon the establishment of a military despotism.

Although in South Carolina Governor Pickens had actually issued the original proclamation of martial law over Charleston, thereby indicating

[1] O. R., Ser. i, Vol. XV, pp. 771–72.

all confidence in the President,[1] there presently began to appear signs of suspicion and fear in that state. On June 22 James Campbell complained to General Cooper that "the old laws and tribunals have been suspended at one brush in Charleston," and that new ones would have to be set up or "there would be none save the *sit justitia* of the general commanding or his provost."[2] About a month later Governor Pickens, who had begun to share in the uneasiness and suspicion, urged the President to restore the civil jurisdiction immediately.[3] The signs of discontent became so evident in South Carolina that Davis wrote Pemberton to restore the civil authorities to "their uninterrupted functions" just as soon as it could be done with safety.[4]

The Georgia group probably voiced the opposition with more vigor than any others. On July 14, 1862, General Toombs wrote Stephens that "Davis and his Jannissaries—the regular army—conspire for the destruction of all who will not bend to them, and avail themselves of the public danger to aid them in their selfish

[1] O. R., Ser. 1, Vol. XIV, pp. 491–92. [3] *Ibid.*, p. 598.
[2] *Ibid.*, pp. 570–71. [4] *Ibid.*, pp. 593, 598.

and infamous schemes."[1] A few weeks later he wrote his friend Burwell, of Virginia, that the "real control of our affairs is narrowing down constantly into the hands of Davis and the old army." He considered this virtual slavery and he was convinced "that the road to liberty for the white man does not lie through slavery."[2] On September 1, 1862, Governor Brown sent Alexander Stephens a message congratulating him upon the decided stand he had taken against the declaration of martial law throughout the country and especially in Atlanta. Brown wrote:

It seems military men are assuming the whole powers of government to themselves and setting at defiance constitutions, laws, state rights, and every principle of civil liberty, and that our people, engrossed in the struggle with the enemy, are disposed to submit to these bold usurpations tending to military despotism without murmur, much less resistence . . . . . I fear we have more to apprehend from military despotism than from subjugation by the enemy."[3]

Then, in his message to the Georgia legislature on November 6, Brown denounced the suspen-

[1] *Toombs, Stephens, Cobb Correspondence, American Historical Association Report*, 1911, II, 601 (cited henceforth as *Toombs, Stephens, Cobb Correspondence*).

[2] *Toombs, Stephens, Cobb Correspondence*, pp. 628–29.

[3] *Ibid.*, p. 605.

sion of the writ and the proclamation of martial law as unconstitutional. He said: "It places the liberty of every citizen of the Confederacy at the mercy of the President, who may imprison any citizen under this order without legal warrant or authority and no court dare interfere to liberate the captive when the imprisonment is illegal." Atlanta, he said, had been placed under martial law with a military governor, and he considered "this and like proceedings on the part of the Confederate officers not only high-handed usurpation, depending for their authority upon military power without the shadow of constitutional right, but which, if acquiesced in by this state, tend to the subversion of the government and the sovereignty of the state and of the individual rights of the citizen."[1]

Stephens expressed the firm conviction that when General Bragg declared martial law in Atlanta he had overstepped the law and constitution by many strides. Bragg, he said, had no more authority to appoint a civil governor of a city, as he had done in Atlanta under a declara-

[1] *Confederate Records of Georgia*, II, 305–7.

tion of martial law, than he himself had, and that was no more right than an ordinary street-walker of Atlanta had. Further, he said, the civil governor of Atlanta had no more power "than if the appointment had been made by a street-walker." He denounced martial law as being absolutely unknown to the Constitution. Congress might suspend the writ, always subject to strict safeguards, one of which was the right of trial in a civil court by a jury of one's peers. Martial law as established in Atlanta was, he asserted, "a palpable usurpation" of powers not contemplated by the Constitution.[1]

The opposition to the establishment of martial law soon was felt in Congress. On August 25, 1862, the irrepressible H. S. Foote, now of Tennessee but once of Mississippi, the deadly foe of Davis, offered a resolution in the House that the judiciary committee be instructed to inquire whether any further legislation was necessary to check the abuse of the law by those intrusted with the enforcement of martial law;

[1] *Rebellion Record*, I, Supplement, 675–76; Jones, *Diary*, I, 163; Henry Cleveland, *Life of Alexander Hamilton Stephens with Letters and Speeches*, pp. 747–49 (cited henceforth as Cleveland, *Stephens*).

also to inquire whether it was true that some of the military commanders had assumed the authority to declare martial law without the sanction of the President. He also desired the committee to suggest what punishment "should be provided for so serious a violation of the rights of our citizens."[1]

The next day, in the Senate, Semmes, of Louisiana, introduced a resolution that the Committee on the Judiciary be directed to inquire into the necessity for further legislation to restrain the military officers within the limits of the Constitution in their exercise of power assumed under color of the act suspending the writ of habeas corpus.[2] On September 10 Haynes, from Tennessee, asked that a law be passed to the effect that no military commander should suspend or abridge freedom of speech; that any person not belonging to the army and navy arrested while the writ of habeas corpus was suspended should not be tried or punished except by the regular civil tribunals upon presentment by grand jury; and that the person or officer making the arrest must set forth in the order of ar-

[1] *Journal of the Confederate Congress*, V, 313.　　[2] *Ibid.*, II, 237.

166

rest the cause and nature of the accusation against such citizens and report the arrest to the President, who in turn should, at stated intervals, report the matter to Congress. Haynes concluded with the assertion that martial law was unknown to the Constitution and that the officers who had proclaimed it should be punished.[1] Senator Oldham, of Texas, expressed the opinion that the war department had no power to vest provost marshals with any authority whatsoever over citizens not belonging to the army, or to police towns or cities in any of the Confederate states, and that all such attempts by the President or his military commanders were unauthorized and illegal. Further, the war department had no constitutional or lawful right to limit or restrict the exercise of the jurisdiction of the civil courts, and that all orders tending so to restrict the courts were illegal and mere assumptions of power.[2] Semmes wished to emphasize Oldham's contention by the assertion that "the military law of the Confederate states is by the Constitution and enactments of Congress limited to the land and naval forces and

[1] *Ibid.*, p. 271.   [2] *Ibid.*, p. 326.

militia when in actual service, and that martial law is unknown to the Constitution."[1] Finally on October 8, resolutions embodying the sentiment of Oldham and Semmes were passed.[2]

Meanwhile the House had been investigating the declaration of martial law by General Hindman in Arkansas, and had dragged that general and the whole war department over the coals and denounced them for their unwarranted assumption of power.[3]

The gist of the whole matter was that a large part of Congress and the state officials and other leaders believed that the President and his generals had assumed more power than was granted them either by the Constitution or the law of April 19, 1862. On the other hand, the President and his subordinates, backed by a great part of the members of Congress and the state officers, believed that if an error had been committed it was due not to wilful violation of the law, but to a misconstruction of the act of April 19, and to an honest desire to save the country, as in the case of Hindman's and Van Dorn's proclama-

[1] *Journal of the Confederate Congress*, II, 394-95.
[2] *Ibid.*, 444. [3] *Ibid.*, V, 333, 356.

tions of martial law. In order to obviate any further misconception of the power granted by the law and to clear up all confusion as to the meaning of the suspension of the writ of habeas corpus and of martial law, the House instructed its Committee of the Judiciary to make a study of the meaning and applications of these terms and report back to the House on its conclusions.

On September 13 the committee rendered its report. The origin of martial law—as understood by the English-speaking peoples—the report set forth, was in the ancient prerogative of the king, "who was absolute over the army in the field and over the life of every person attached to the army in time of war." His commands were law to the army and to the courts of the marshals; in other words, "absolute power administered by military courts in summary proceedings constituted martial law." Furthermore, the king had claimed and often exercised the right of extending martial law over the civil population in times of war or insurrections, and "it was generally admitted, by those who condemned as well as those who invoked its exercise, that martial law, wherever and whenever it

could lawfully prevail, had the effect to insti-
tute arbitary power and the jurisdiction of
courts martial." But martial law, as applicable
to the army and navy, had been superseded in
England and America by a system of regulations
enacted by the legislature, known as military
law, the only law "now known as applicable to
the government of the army." As to martial
laws being applicable to citizens not in the army,
the report pointed out, in a country governed by
a written constitution "it is impossible that martial law in its ancient and customary sense can
exist." Neither in peace nor war could the citizens be subject to any power inconsistent with
the constitution or laws. There were, however
a few things authorized by the Constitution
"which were done three centuries ago under the
name of martial law." For example, the writ of
habeas corpus could be suspended, "but to suspend the writ is not to establish martial law
with its summary proceedings and absolute
power. Although when the writ is suspended the
citizen may be restrained of his liberty, he can
be tried and punished only according to the laws
of the land." After drawing the distinction thus

between martial law and the suspense of the writ of habeas corpus, the Committee recommended in their report that a definite, clear-cut law with no ambiguous phrases be substituted for the one just about to expire.[1]

2. SECOND LAW, OCTOBER 13, 1862 TO FEBRUARY 13, 1863

This opposition in and out of Congress—though ofttimes unreasonable and unjust it might be—had a marked effect upon the use that the administration made of its power to suspend the writ of habeas corpus. Although the next law, passed October 13, 1862, was a virtual re-enactment of the one just expired[2]—enacted in spite of the states-right opposition—the writ was suspended in fewer places, and the war department was very careful to warn the generals that the suspension of the writ of habeas corpus was not martial law, as they had heretofore interpreted; that its suspense "is not to be considered as authorizing the trial by military

[1] For the entire report, see *Journal of Confederate Congress*, V, 373–77.

[2] For the law, see O. R., Ser. 4, Vol. II, p. 121; see also *Journal of Confederate Congress*, II, 481; V, 560.

courts of civilians for the offenses committed, but only as holding them in duress."[1] Furthermore, the war department, under the direction of the President, administered a severe rebuke to Hèbert, Van Dorn, and Hindman for presuming to establish martial law or suspend the writ without authority from the President, and issued General Order No. 66 annuling all unauthorized proclamations on the question of the suspension of the writ.[2] Still, the lack of communication between the various parts of the Confederacy and the rapidly changing local conditions calling for prompt remedy to prevent disaster, on the one hand,[3] and the petty meanness of arrogant, self-important, subordinate officers on the other,[4] resulted in a few cases in an overstepping of the law.

But the act itself, as tending toward consolidation and threatening state rights, as well

[1] O. R., Ser. 1, Vol. XV, p. 859.

[2] *Ibid.*, Ser. 4, Vol. II, p. 83; *ibid.*, Ser. 1, Vol. IX, pp. 735-36; *ibid.*, Vol. XVII, Part II, p. 694; *ibid.*, XIII, 38-44, 835-36, 886.

[3] *Ibid.*, Ser. 1, Vol. XV, pp. 220, 829, 974, 1018, 1021; *ibid.*, XXVI, Part II, p. 16.

[4] Stephenson, *Day of the Confederacy*, pp. 116-18; Schwab, p. 191; Jones, *Diary*, I, 157-59.

as the occasional abuse of the law, inherited the opposition to the law that had just expired. H. S. Foote continued his efforts in Congress to discredit the President and the army;[1] and Zebulon Vance, the newly elected anti-administration governor of North Carolina, swung the state into a position of violent opposition to the suspension of the writ of habeas corpus. On November 11 he wrote Davis a strong protest against the arrest and imprisonment without trial of forty persons merely suspected of disloyalty. "As governor of the state of which they are citizens," he said, "it becomes my duty to see that they are protected in whatever rights pertain to them. First among them is the undoubted right of trial for their alleged offenses."[2] A few days later, without waiting for a response to his letter, Vance laid the matter before the assembly in a message that fairly bristled with hostility toward the administration. How long these men whom the Confederate government had arrested would remain incarcerated without trial "no one can say but those who apprehended them." What

[1] *Journal of the Confederate Congress*, VI, 516, 544.

[2] O. R., Ser. 1, Vol. LI, Part II, pp. 644-45.

their guilt really consisted in he did not know, but he knew this: "They were not arrested by lawful process." As citizens of North Carolina, he declared, they were entitled under the Constitution to a speedy trial by a jury of their peers, and to be confronted by their accusers. The law suspending the writ in all cases of arrest by the Confederate authorities, under which these persons had been apprehended, was a dangerous grant of power. "If this be once admitted," he said, "no man is safe from the power of one individual"—a power he was "unwilling to see intrusted to any living man." To submit to it would be establishing a dangerous precedent. He could see "little good, but a vast tide of inflowing evil from these inordinate stretches of military power." A free republic that cast its freedom off in time of danger would soon cast it off forever. Finally, he looked to the legislature to provide legal safeguards against such usurpations of power.[1] The Governor's message found a responsive chord in the assembly and throughout North Carolina. The next year, 1863, after the law suspending the writ had ex-

[1] O. R., Ser. 4, Vol. II, p. 188; Schwab, p. 190.

pired, the supreme court of the state decided that it could issue the writ in the case of those arrested and still held by the Confederate government under authority of the act that expired in February, 1863. As a result of this decision there was a serious conflict between Confederate and state authorities. A soldier who had been discharged, probably by Judge Pearson at Chambers, on the grounds of being above age, was arrested by the Confederate authorities and again released upon the writ of habeas corpus proceedings in the state courts. No sooner had he regained his freedom than he was again placed in custody by the Confederate authorities. This was more than the angry Governor could stand, so he sent a detachment of state troops who "recaptured" the much harassed soldier.[1] Other similar difficulties arose that caused much bad feeling between the local and Confederate officials,[2] and indignation meetings were held all over the state.[3] North Carolina outstripped all

[1] Schwab, *Confederate States*, p. 191.

[2] *Ibid.*, *Montgomery Daily Mail*, July 2, 1862; O. R., Ser. 1, Vol. LI; Part II, p. 709.

[3] Schwab, p. 191.

other states, having left even Georgia behind at this point.

With the head thus gained by the opposition, the administration forces were unable at the time to pass another law to take the place of the one that expired on February 13, 1863.[1]

3. THIRD LAW, FEBRUARY 15, 1864, EXPIRING AUGUST 1, 1864

However, after the space of a year, the President was able, by a very urgent message,[2] February 3, 1864, to rally the factious congressmen so as to pass an act to suspend the writ.[3] This law left nothing to the discretion of the President, but suspended the writ of habeas corpus throughout the Confederacy in cases of treason, conspiracy to overthrow the government, desertion, spying, giving aid to the enemy, bridge-burning, wrecking railroads, etc. A commission was to be appointed by the president in each state to investigate the cases of all persons so arrested

[1] *Journal of the Confederate Congress*, VI, 7, 74, 151, 155, 318, 319, 352, 516, 544, 621; *ibid.*, III, 517, 518, 546, 601, 602.

[2] *Ibid.*, VI, 744-46.

[3] *Ibid.*, pp. 756, 757, 761-64, 805-7, 822, 845, 847, 866, 868; *ibid.*, III, 669-71, 673, 674, 684, 692, 693, 701-4, 708-12, 722, 751, 796.

and detained in order that they might be discharged or given speedy trial, if improperly held. The act was to remain in force ninety days after the next meeting of Congress—that is, till August 1, 1864.[1] This act precipitated one of the bitterest, and in some respects most disastrous, conflicts of the whole war between Confederate and state authorities.

North Carolina, not without reason, felt herself to be the special target of this last act. Holden, a prominent newspaper editor, and Governor Vance were both more or less in favor of peace—Holden really headed a movement for a separate peace on any terms. Public meetings had been held that made anti-administration and anti-Confederate demonstrations. So North Carolina at once concluded that the law was aimed at her. On February 9, 1864, while the act was still pending in Congress, Vance protested to Davis against its passage and its application to North Carolina. He wrote the President that he understood that the law was for the special benefit of North Carolina; and, while

[1] For the law, see O. R., Ser. 4, Vol. III, pp. 203–4; cf. Schwab, p. 187.

he was sure it would do no good to try to dissuade the Confederate authorities from passing it, he would not hold himself guiltless if he failed to warn the Confederate government that it was attempting a dangerous thing in suspending the writ in his state. He imagined, he said, that the people would submit to the law if it were within the limits of the Constitution—which he doubted—but on the contrary, if it were adjudged "to be in violation of that instrument and revolutionary in itself, it would be resisted." He advised the President, in case the law passed, "to be chary of the exercise of the powers" with which it would vest him. He urged that he hold it over the heads of the discontented as a threat and a possible punishment rather than make actual use of the power, thus shocking "all worshippers of the common law . . . . by hurling freemen into sheriffless dungeons for opinion's sake." Finally he seemed to lose his self-restraint, and poured forth a torrent of abuse upon the head of the President for his treatment of North Carolinians and his attitude of suspicion toward that state—in fact, he blamed Davis for conscription, impressment, favoritism in appointing to office other than North Carolinians, and especially old unionists; he blamed him for everything in such language as only Vance or Brown could command.[1] President Davis replied that he was not at all eager to make use of the power granted him—in fact, arbitrary measures were not at all congenial to his nature—but that "should the occasion unhappily arise when the public safety demanded their employment" he would not flinch from his duty; and that he would rely "for support on the mass of good people of North Carolina, in spite of the blandishments of those who would persuade them that their liberties are endangered, not by the wicked invaders of their country, but by their own government and their own fellow-citizens." He denied Vance's accusation that he had looked upon North Carolina with suspicion. On the other hand, he assured him, he did not entertain "aught but respect and admiration for the people of North Carolina and her gallant sons who have on the battle fields of this war won for her so glorious a name." But he did "suspect a knot of traitors who have been

[1] O. R., Ser. 1, Vol. LI, Part II, pp. 818-20.

179

conspiring at home while the mass of the state's true sons were at their posts of duty in the army."[1] The reply was, on the whole, moderate, in view of the stinging abuse that Vance had heaped upon his head. Like Joe Brown, however, Vance was not willing for his opponent to have the last word, even if it were a mild word, so on March 9 he wrote the President a letter more insinuating and insulting than ever, going over the many old points and bringing in new ones.[2] Davis was unwilling to continue a controversy that so compromised his position and self-respect, so after replying to Vance in a letter of March 31, he said, "I must beg that a correspondence so unprofitable in its character, and which was not initiated by me, may here end, and that your future communications may be restricted to such matters as may require official action."[3] This bitter personal controversy between a governor and the President, with its unsatisfactory settlement, was ominous.

Nor was the North Carolina legislature behind in its opposition to the law. It passed reso-

[1] O. R., Ser. 1, Vol. LI, Part II, pp. 824-27.
[2] *Ibid.*, pp. 830-33.   [3] *Ibid.*, pp. 844-46.

lution after resolution condemning the act as a violation of all the fundamental principles of freedom and liberty, as superseding civil with military authority and overthrowing state sovereignty—in short, as the senate expressed it, "instead of a confederacy of free and sovereign states we have established a most powerful consolidated military despotism." The legislature finally passed a law making it compulsory for the judges to issue the writ of habeas corpus.[1] With such a splendid background of discontent, Judge Pearson, after deciding that the law conscripting principals of substitutes was not constitutional, proceeded to issue the writ of habeas corpus to all those reluctant gentlemen who desired one;[2] and to anyone else in the army on the flimsiest pretext.[3] With the Governor using his militia to uphold these decisions of Pearson the law of February 15, 1864, was at times almost a nullity in North Carolina.

Mississippi soon joined the hostile ranks; its legislature passed resolutions condemning the

[1] Schwab, pp. 191–92.

[2] O. R., Ser. 4, Vol. III, pp. 176–77, 197–98, 200–201.

[3] *Ibid.*, pp. 238, 256, 375–76, 425–28, 530, 555–56; *ibid.*, Ser. 1, Vol. LI, Part II, p. 709.

act suspending the writ,[1] and her congressmen at Richmond joined the anti-administration fight.

In Louisiana, where civil government was virtually non-existent, the military commanders, under cover of the law suspending the writ, took matters into their own hands and attempted to restore order and inject a degree of morale into the demoralized population. Trading with the enemy was the order of the day; spies walked openly and men were wavering in their loyalty. So there was really every excuse for a strong hand—even if the law did not cover the case. But the people thus affected did not welcome the iron rule of the colonels and the officious provost marshals, and there arose a protest against it. Preston Pond, who was the Governor's representative, wrote the Governor on May 8 that he had sent a protest to the President against the high-handed and lawless manner in which officers had violated all rights of property and person. The evils which he had pointed out to Davis were enormous. "The lives, liberties, and property of our citizens are disposed of with the same

[1] *Journal of the Confederate Congress*, VII, 55; *ibid.*, IV, 34.

facility of subordinate military officers as if each of them was a hereditary despot in the district or department assigned to his command." Citizens of Louisiana, he had complained, were taken into Mississippi and executed without trial. "I am at loss," he said, "to know by what authority any military commander of whatever grade, from President to the corporal, assumes to annul the Constitution; to move across the lines of state sovereignty as if they did not exist, and by simple military orders deprive our citizens of life." He believed that this invasion of the constitutional authority of the civil tribunals was "a common portent of revolution" and civil decay and called "for the most sleepless vigilance." He regretted that "military men cannot keep in view the great cardinal principles of our government and preserve the harmony of its structure and action, even through the convulsions of war"; and he predicted that the destruction of state sovereignty and the abandonment of the original principles would "excite a bloodier revolution than the present."[1]

But the best-organized and most far-reaching

[1] O. R., Ser. 4, Vol. III, pp. 398–400.

opposition, as heretofore, came from the Georgia group. Vice-President Stephens, who spent most of his time in Georgia, was at the moment perhaps the most influential man in the whole Confederacy. There were more discontented people than contented people in the country, and Stephens, who was an agitator and an apostle of discontent, rallied the disgruntled elements to his call. He was the veritable "wet nurse" of the Georgia group and "mothered" the state-rights faction throughout the Confederacy. He affected to have no personal enmity toward the President,[1] claiming to confine himself to political opposition. As a matter of fact, this most interesting man was very human and could not thus soar above the clouds in the lighter medium reserved for the gods; on the contrary, he harbored as much concentrated venom in his diminutive frame as one could well imagine in a Georgia rattlesnake, and his dislike for Davis was far from being a mere political difference—it was thoroughly mixed with the personal. He it was who first detected the symptoms of military despotism creeping out from Richmond. He had at-

[1] O. R. Ser. 4, Vol. III, pp. 278-81.

tacked the suspension of the writ as early as 1862, and many things had happened since that time to confirm his suspicious mind in the belief that Davis was aiming at absolute power. So when the law of February 15, 1864, was pending in Congress he planned immediate defiance and the overthrow of the administration—and possibly the overthrow of the Confederacy—as the safest thing for the people's liberties.

Let us see how he, with the aid of his brother Linton, Robert Toombs, and his understudy, Joseph E. Brown pulled the political wires. This group had, as usual, been in constant and intimate correspondence just before the passage of the law suspending the writ, and they had planned their campaign against it. So on February 13, when it was assured that the bill would become a law, Brown wrote Stephens to meet him at his brother Linton's where the three could "compare notes on the subject" about which they had "lately corresponded," and prepare the message Brown would deliver at the special session of the legislature to be called in March.[1] On February 20 Brown set a definite date, the fol-

[1] *Toombs, Stephens, Cobb Correspondence*, p. 633.

lowing Thursday, for the time at which Alexander Stephens was to meet him "to compare notes" and prepare his message. "The great wrong which you anticipated," he wrote Stephens, "has been done by Congress, and I confess I contemplate with horror the suspension of the habeas corpus. Every state in the Confederacy should denounce and condemn the wicked act."[1] After the conference with the two Stephenses, Brown called his legislature together and delivered his message, which was full of hatred of the administration and hostility to the entire Confederate policy, with particular emphasis upon the military despotism portended by the late act suspending the writ of habeas corpus.[2] The message was so evidently the handiwork of Stephens—he was a much abler man than Brown—that Ben Hill, who had been invited to take part in the fight against the law, wrote Stephens: "Governor Brown can never pay you in kind for the great benefit you have bestowed upon him. . . . . His only trouble can be [that] the footprints are too plain not to be recog-

[1] *Toombs, Stephens, Cobb Correspondence*, p. 633.

[2] *Confederate Records of Georgia*, II, 608–18.

nized."[1] Stephens made no bones about its being his handiwork: he wrote H. V. Johnson that he had "advised it from stem to stern."[2]

While "comparing notes" at Linton's home before the legislature convened, Vice-President Stephens had also guided his brother's hand in the preparation of the famous resolutions in favor of peace and against the suspension of the writ of habeas corpus. As to his responsibility for these resolutions, he afterward wrote H. V. Johnson they were not drawn up by himself, "but they were prepared by Linton after full consultation."[3] These resolutions Linton introduced at the proper moment after Brown, by his message of March 10, 1864, had carried the administration position by storm.[4] Hereupon, on March 16, Alexander Stephens came to the support of the resolutions and Brown's message with a stirring address before the legislature, calculated to arouse sufficient strength to pass the resolutions. Stephen's speech was long,

[1] *Toombs, Stephens, Cobb Correspondence*, pp. 634–35.

[2] O. R., Ser. 4, Vol. III, pp. 278–81.

[3] *Ibid.*, p. 279.

[4] For resolutions see O. R., Ser. 4, Vol. III, pp. 234–35.

but powerful and to the point. He did not question the right of Congress to suspend the privilege of the writ, but he attacked this law on the ground that it gave the President judicial power to make arrests without oath of probable cause, in short, "to authorize illegal and unconstitutional arrests." He contended that if the writ were legally suspended its only effect would be to prevent a person's being released before trial—either on bail or for lack of evidence. Another insidious danger of the law was its withholding the privilege of a judicial hearing for men claiming exemption from military service. This would result in all persons of whatever age or condition being thrust into the service if Davis so wished. Finally and most important, this law, together with the conscript law of February, 1864, put absolute power in the President's hands. The conscript law put all between seventeen and fifty under Davis's control. Then the habeas corpus law conferred upon him:

The power to order the arrest and imprisonment of any man, woman, and child in the Confederacy on a bare charge, unsupported by oath, of any act for which arrests are allowed to be made. Could the whole country be more completely under the power and control of one man. . . . ? Could dictatorial power be more complete? In this connection consider also the strong appeals that have been made for some time past by leading journals, openly, for a dictator. Coming events often cast their shadows before. Could art or ingenuity have devised a shorter or surer cut to that end than the whole policy adopted by the last Congress?

Shortly after this speech Stephens wrote H. V. Johnson: "I had but little hope, when this measure first passed, that we should ever again have constitutional liberty upon this continent —from that day till this I have had but little hope."[1]

That the Governor's message, Linton's resolutions, and Alexander Stephen's speech were meant for a wide audience was soon evident. Brown sent copies of his message and the resolutions to the captain of each company in every Georgia regiment in the Confederate service, and a copy to the clerk of every county court within the lines of the Confederacy.[2] As to Stephen's speech, Brown was determined that it should be

[1] *Toombs, Stephens, Cobb Correspondence*, p. 639, footnote; Cleveland, *Stephens*, pp. 761–86; *ibid.*, pp. 793–95.

[2] *Toombs, Stephens, Cobb Correspondence*, pp. 639–40.

circulated at all costs. Not being an official speech, it could not be printed at public expense, so he paid part of the expenses himself and the rest was paid by certain private individuals who were interested in overthrowing the policy of the administration.[1] So on April 12 he wrote Stephens that he would send the lieutenant of each company of all the Georgia regiments a copy, so that if the captain, to whom he had sent the message and Linton's resolutions, was against him, the lieutenant might be friendly and would see that the company was acquainted with the stand that Georgia had taken. He had sent his message to the clerk of each county, he wrote, and now he would send Stephen's speech to the sheriff of each county in the Confederacy so that "if one is not read, then it is probable the other will be."[2]

The effect of this organized propaganda was overwhelming. J. L. M. Curry, of Alabama, who had been recently appointed as one of the commissioners to carry into effect certain provisions of the act suspending the writ, wrote Secretary

[1] *Toombs, Stephens, Cobb Correspondence*, pp. 639–40.

[2] *Ibid.*, pp. 640–41.

Seddon that the execution of the act in Georgia would be practically impossible, "owing to the opposition of Governor Brown, the Vice-President, and other prominent men in Georgia. Nothing, he said, had appeared in the newspapers in defense of the law, but scores of the malcontents had done all they could to make the law, the President, and the Secretary of War odious.[1]

In a meeting of the governors of the states east of the Mississippi, October 17, 1864, a resolution virtually condemning the suspension of the writ of habeas corpus was adopted, and thus practically every state was on record as being hostile to any form of martial law.[2]

With the states in a condition of virtual rebellion against the administration, the state-rights faction in Congress attempted to repeal the act of February 15, but were unable to muster enough strength, in view of the fact that the President would veto any law repealing said act.[3] But when the law expired in August all efforts

[1] O. R., Ser. 1, Vol. LII, Part II, p. 648.

[2] *Ibid.*, Ser. 4, Vol. III, pp. 735–36.

[3] *Journal of the Confederate Congress*, VII, 12, 54, 55, 57, 58, 65, 78, 80–83, 101–11.

to pass another law suspending the writ were futile. The President called in vain. The committee in Congress selected to reply to his message summed up their reason for not passing another law in the following words: "The states of North Carolina, Georgia, and Mississippi had expressed, through their legislatures, great repugnance to the last legislation of Congress suspending the writ, and a large portion of the people throughout the country was arrayed against the policy of that legislation."[1]

Besides contributing largely to the breakdown of the morale of the people and the army, this controversy between the states and the Confederacy, as we have seen, resulted in defeating the efforts of the administration party to pass a law suspending the writ during the entire year of 1863—the year of Vicksburg and Gettysburg—and during the time from August 1, 1864, until the end of the war.

Let us examine the conditions that made the suspension of the writ indispensable, the conditions which could have been to a great extent

[1] *Journal of the Confederate Congress*, VII, 81–82; O. R., Ser. 4, Vol. III, p. 1150; Schwab, pp. 189–90.

alleviated if the Confederate government had been given a free hand in suspending the writ, as the United States had been given, and which helped materially in overthrowing the Confederacy. In the first place, the writ was used by state judges under the influence of state-rights governors to destroy the Confederate army. Judge Pearson issued the writ in behalf of principals of substitutes[1] to soldiers in actual service who were appointed or elected to petty state offices,[2] and finally he scrupled not at all to issue the writ for deserters from the Confederate army.[3] On March 29, 1864, Commissioner Thomas Bragg reported that at Salisbury, North Carolina, alone there were about 120 cases of this kind.[4]

In Virginia during the last year of the war the discharge of soldiers and conscripts by means of the writ of habeas corpus was as great as in North Carolina. General Early wrote Secretary Seddon on November 27 that if the writ of habe-

[1] *Montgomery Daily Mail*, July 2, 1863; O.R., Ser. 4, Vol. III, pp. 176–77, 197–98, 200–201.

[2] *Ibid.*, pp. 375–76, 425–28, 555–56.

[3] *Ibid.*, Ser. 1, Vol. LI, Part II, p. 709.

[4] *Ibid.*, Ser. 4, Vol. III, p. 256.

as corpus was not suspended, Judge Thomas
of the Virginia bench, would discharge all his
men.[1] But Thomas was not the only one who
seemed bent upon the destruction of the army:
Judges Fulton, Meredith, and Halyburton were
all engaged in a similar activity. Two of the
most outstanding cases of Judge Fulton were
those of John C. Kinzer and John Surface, privates in the Fifty-fourth Virginia Regiment.
These men made bids for mail routes at the absurd salary of one cent and one-fourth cent,
respectively, per annum, and were awarded the
jobs. The officers of their regiment offered to
apply for a discharge for them, but they refused
the proffer: they were unwilling to be bothered
by such red tape, for they had already made arrangements with Judge Fulton for a discharge
through habeas corpus proceedings. Presently
the Judge issued the writs and sent an officer all
the way into Tennessee, several hundred miles,
to execute the writs. The record does not show,
but judging from other cases the colonel of the
regiment or at least the captain of the company
in which these men were enlisted was forced to

[1] O. R., Ser. 1, Vol. XLIII, Part II, pp. 924–25.

194

return the men in person over this great distance or face a charge of contempt of court. However, the men were surrendered by their organization —though the writs issued in Virginia could not be served legally in Tennessee—and Judge Fulton discharged them when they were brought before him.[1] Judge Halyburton made a similar discharge of three men in one day.[2] The discharge of Thomas Varden was, according to the report of Captain Thorburn, one of the many similar cases sued out before Judge Meredith, and further illustrates how the state courts served as a vast "leak" in the military system of the Confederacy. Varden, an able-bodied soldier, obtained an election as justice of the peace, whereupon Judge Meredith issued the writ of habeas corpus in his behalf. Captain Thorburn, the Confederate officer appointed by General W. H. Taylor to make return to the writ, traveled to Richmond along with his man Varden only to have the latter discharged by the Judge.[3]

December, 1863, General Greer of the trans-Mississippi department reported that the deci-

[1] *Ibid.*, Ser. 4, Vol. III, pp. 71–72.
[2] *Ibid.*, p. 73.   [3] *Ibid.*, pp. 659–60.

sions of certain judicial officers in the department had seriously crippled the whole military system in that region. "It seems," he said, "to be a favorite scheme of some of the Texas judges to override the Confederate laws and to discharge from service in the army any and all who apply to them for relief." These judges had power, he said, to do great harm, for any judge in Texas could issue the writ for the whole state, and soldiers would know to whom to make their application. He named two judges who were especially guilty of injuring the army—W. P. Hill and B. W. Gray. Judge Hill had decided that all state officers, even down to the grade of deputy county clerk, were either exempt from military service if elected before entering, or were subject to discharge if elected after enlistment. Greer complained that this would result in utter disbandment of the army if persisted in; for, he said, "the power of the . . . . clerks and sheriffs to appoint deputies is unlimited: they may appoint every man in the county if they choose, and under Judge Hill's decision they would all be exempt."

But Hill did not confine himself to deputy

clerks and deputy sheriffs. Greer cited an instance where he had discharged an overseer who had made false affidavits, sworn to be untrue by his neighbors, after the overseer had paid Hill's son 500 bushels of corn to sue for a writ in his behalf before his father. He pointed out a few cases tried before Judge Gray which were even worse. One A. M. Walker, who had been a physician but who had quit his profession to become speculator, was arrested by the Confederate authorities and put in the army, whereupon Gray issued a writ of habeas corpus to the officer in command to appear before him with said Walker and show reasons why Walker was detained. Greer appointed an eminent attorney to represent the government, but the Judge, in order that he might "make assurance doubly sure," gave the attorney the wrong information as to the day on which the case was to be brought up. The result was that the attorney did not appear at the trial, and the petitioner was discharged in default of witnesses against him. Greer said that after this experience he had made a special point of asking Gray and Hill to notify his attorney whenever similar cases came up, but that Gray soon afterward discharged two others in like fashion. These cases, he said, although the regular term of court was in session, "were tried not in the open court but at chambers, without the knowledge of the counsel whom I had employed, although he was in attendance upon the court."[1]

It is impossible to estimate the damage done by this "leak" in the Confederate military system, but it was evidently considerable, for on February 1, 1864, President Davis remarked that "in some of the states civil process has been brought to bear with disastrous efficiency upon the army";[2] and General Lee wrote Secretary of War Seddon, September 10, 1864, that as a result of the use of the writ of habeas corpus "the drain upon the strength of the army by exemption of civil officers, postmasters, clerks, and mail-carriers is more than it can bear."[3]

But the discharge of conscripts, war-weary soldiers, and deserters was only one part of the evils resulting from not suspending the writ of habeas corpus and giving the Confederacy a

[1] O. R., Ser. 1, Vol. XXVI, Part II, pp. 493–95.
[2] Ibid., Ser. 4, Vol. III, pp. 67–70.   [3] Ibid., p. 660.

freer hand after the spring of 1863. Through great parts of Mississippi, Louisiana, Arkansas, Tennessee, Georgia, Alabama, and Virginia civil government had utterly disappeared, with the exception of an occasional judge sitting at chambers and doing more damage than good. In these war-ridden states a strong hand was needed, for in the absence of any government floating gangs of deserters, draft-dodgers, tories, cutthroats, and disloyal men ravaged the country defying with organized skill all who attempted to bring them to account. But the state-rights party would not allow the Confederate government an opportunity to establish order, preferring to see the whole social structure crash down in chaos rather than have a few men arrested and held without speedy trial. In a soil engendered by such conditions, treason and disloyalty grew like mushrooms and the morale of the people decayed as rapidly and by 1864 disloyal peace societies soon affected over half the population in portions of Mississippi, North Carolina, Virginia, Georgia, and Alabama. The leaders of these societies were known, yet the writ of habeas corpus invariably freed them on the grounds of insufficient evidence. Spies and bridge-burners went unmolested and gave aid and comfort to the enemy in broad daylight. President Davis, in his message to Congress, February, 1864, said that on one occasion, a party of men had been planting a torpedo in the James River and certain parties on shore were detected giving signals to the enemy and piloting him to a place of observation. These men had been arrested but were immediately discharged through habeas corpus proceedings, for "although there was moral certainty of their guilt it could not be proved by competent testimony." Another man, he said, had been arrested for disloyalty and twice brought before a military commission, each time acknowledging his hostility to the Confederate cause, but each time he had been discharged on a writ of habeas corpus by the civil authorities from lack of proper evidence. Always it was thus. "Again and again," said Davis, "such persons have been arrested and as often discharged by the civil authorities because the government could not procure testimony from within the enemy's lines."[1]

[1] O. R., Ser. 4, Vol. III, pp. 67–70.

Another matter which demanded nothing less than military control in order to escape from its undermining influence was the widespread trading with the enemy. Such a condition seems always to be a harbinger of collapse, a sure sign of complete breakdown in morale. It is both cause and effect of defeat. Throughout Mississippi, Louisiana, northern Alabama, and parts of Virginia during the last year of the war the people were interested in nothing except selling cotton to the enemy and obtaining greenbacks or gold. F. H. Hatch, the collector of customs at an important point in the Southwest, wrote Secretary of the Treasury Trenholme, September, 1864, that "this population may be divided into three classes: those who have been directly or indirectly concerned in this trade; those who desire to be so but are unable, and those who abstain from considerations of loyalty and respect for law, the latter being an honored and almost invisible minority." At first, he wrote, he could by "the mere moral force of office stop a whole train of wagons" carrying cotton through the lines, but now to "such an extent has the demoralization increased" that the same attempt would have endangered his life. "No law or regulation can be enforced except by the exhibition of military force."[1]

With such conditions resulting from failure to empower the President to suspend the writ of habeas corpus and to establish martial law in the regions where civil government had been destroyed, it is not a mere coincidence that in 1863 —when there was no law to suspend the writ— was the turning of the tide against the Confederacy; and that after August 1, 1864, when the last act suspending the writ had expired, the fortunes of the South never rose again.[2]

[1] O. R., Ser. 4, Vol. III, pp. 677-78; cf. *ibid.*, pp. 645-51.

[2] President Davis placed probably more importance in the last year of the war upon the suspension of the writ than this chapter has been able to do for fear of exaggeration. In May, 1864, Davis warned Congress, which was attempting to repeal the law, that "it would be perilous if not calamitous to discontinue the suspense" (*Journal of the Confederate Congress*, VII, 81-82); and in the spring of 1865 he again warned Congress of the danger of not suspending the writ. The time had come, he said, "when the suspension of the writ is not simply expedient, but almost indispensable to the successful conduct of the war" (O. R., Ser. 4, Vol. III, p. 1134).

CHAPTER IV
CONSCRIPTION

Most intimately related to the struggle over the suspense of the writ of habeas corpus is the controversy between the states and the Confederate government over conscription. The story of this controversy has been adequately treated by another writer,[1] and only a sketch as far as the narrative of the struggle is concerned will be given. There is one aspect of the subject, however, that permits of further study: the effect of this contest upon the results of the war.

For the sake of clarity and continuity I shall state briefly the chief points of contest between the states and the Confederacy. Governor Brown, of Georgia, along with the Stephenses and Robert Toombs, and Governor Vance, of North Carolina, immediately entered the lists against the policy of conscription. Their chief arguments were: conscription was unnecessary

[1] A. B. Moore, *Conscription and Conflict in the Confederacy*.

and inexpedient—southern men would not submit to the humiliation of being drafted, and the armies could be recruited sufficiently by volunteering; it was unconstitutional because it would destroy the state militia; it would or could enrol the state officers and destroy the state government; and it would take the power of appointing military officers out of the hands of the governor and put it in the hands of the President. Aside from specific violations of the Constitution, it was a violation of the spirit and tendency of that instrument because it placed too much power in the hands of President Davis. Brown and Vance were the leaders, in their respective states, of the opposition during the early years of conscription, and were the only real opponents among the state governors up until the law of February 17, 1864, which had for its aim the transfer of all the effective state troops to the Confederate reserves. After that law was passed practically every state arrayed itself against the central government on the conscription question. Brown and Vance became more obstreperous than ever, while governors such as Milton, of Florida, and Clark, of Mississippi, "kept their mouths shut and sawed wood" and rendered as much damage as their more noisy neighbors.

In the controversy over conscription—aside from general obstruction—the states asserted several claims with great success and corresponding hurt to the Confederacy: the exemption of state officers, militia officers, and state troops. So much for the main points of the narrative. It will be our chief task to point out in detail the numbers actually withdrawn by this wholesale exemption policy of the states. It has already been noted in the chapter on "Local Defense" that there were many able-bodied men who had successfully dodged the Confederate service by smuggling themselves away in the rear ranks of the state organizations for local defense. Their number was legion and it will be unnecessary to give an account of them in this connection. Therefore, it will be possible for us to confine the investigation to the number of state and militia officers exempted by the states' claims.

Governor Brown claimed successfully almost all the state officers—he exempted clerks, deputy clerks, sheriffs, deputy sheriffs, and their deputies, magistrates, notary publics, tax collectors, deputy collectors, and their clerks, judges—in fact Brown exempted any man whom he wished to by attaching him to some shadowy and elusive official position. Even the employees on the state and public railways and factories fell into the category of "state officer."[1] Then he turned to his militia and granted every member a commission who was not already exempt by virtue of being a state officer or on account of physical disability.[2] It was a common saying that "every private in Joe Brown's militia holds an officer's commission,"[3] and this was just about true, for it was pointed out time after time that there were about 3,000 militia officers between the ages of eighteen and forty-five in Brown's militia. Colonel Browne (of the Confederate service) reported 2,751 in November, 1864, as being subject to general service.[4] General Howell Cobb, who was in position to know, placed the number at not less than 3,000 men of military age.[5] The number of

[1] O. R., Ser. 4, Vol. I, pp. 1082–85; *ibid.*, Vol. III, pp. 345–47.

[2] *Ibid.*, Vol. I, pp. 1082–85; *ibid.*, Vol. III, pp. 345–46; *ibid.*, 869–70; *Macon Telegraph*, in *Montgomery Mail*, December 7, 1862.

[3] *Macon Telegraph*, in *Montgomery Mail*, March 31, 1863.

[4] O. R., Ser. 4, Vol. III, pp. 869–70; cf. *ibid.*, pp. 1102–10.

[5] *Ibid.*, pp. 344–49.

men exempted as state or militia officers ranged from 8,000 to 15,000. Colonel Browne reported the number on November 29, 1864, as 5,478 civil officers and 2,751 militia officers.[1] General Cobb about this time estimated the number at over 6,000 county and militia officers, exclusive of state officers and operatives in the factories.[2] President Davis gave the number of able-bodied men in Georgia who were classed as "officers" as 15,000.[3] It is probable that the figures were something more than 8,000 and that Davis was approximately correct, for the numbers reported by Cobb and Colonel Browne were those obtained through the conscription office, which only showed those who had presented their certificates of exemption to the conscription officers. This did not cover anything like the whole body of exempts, as Brown, claiming that a blanket proclamation exempted all officers named therein, never issued a certificate to an officer until that officer was cornered by the Confederate authorities. As Preston said, the 8,000 reported

[1] *Ibid.*, pp. 869–70; cf. *ibid.*, pp. 1102–10.

[2] *Ibid.*, pp. 344–49.

[3] *Rise and Fall of the Confederate Government*, II, 560–66.

was only "progressive" and that as time passed more exempts would show up.[1]

These facts lend much color to the statement of the enrolling officer in Georgia to General Cobb that there were more men, during 1864, between eighteen and forty-five staying at home than had gone from the state into Confederate service during the war.[2]

In Mississippi, during 1864 and 1865, the situation became as bad as in Georgia. Governor Clark quietly asserted his rights to all state and militia officers and refused to be drawn into any controversy.[3] The Governor insisted that his proclamation served as a blanket exemption for the classes of officers mentioned therein, and that no personal certificate from him should be given.[4] Acting on this principle he actually granted only about 200 certificates, which caused the conscription officers to report only that number of officers exempted in Mississippi,[5] when as

[1] See O. R., Ser. 4, Vol. III, p. 867.

[2] Ibid., p. 75; Cobb was unable to believe this until convinced by seeing for himself the great number of men of military age in Georgia.

[3] Ibid., pp. 866–67.

[4] Ibid., p. 866.

[5] Ibid., p. 867; cf. ibid., pp. 1102–3.

a matter of fact he had exempted several thousand men of military age. Brigadier General H.
W. Walter, who made an inspection tour through
Mississippi in November, 1864, complained of
the fact that the bureau reports showed only 204
state exempts when as a matter of common
knowledge there were over 2,300 county, and
nearly 2,000 state officers exempted under the
Governor's proclamation. "This abuse is greater
in Georgia," said General Walter, but, he protested, "that state shows in the conscript reports
the truth, however discreditable. Mississippi en-
joys the benefits but avoids the stigma."[1] These
numbers do not include the militia officers who
must have numbered not less than 2,000, since,
as we have seen in the chapter on local defense,
there were several thousand state militia in
active service. These figures for Mississippi
throw a light upon the reports of the conscript
bureau, which Preston always admitted were
"progressive" and not final. It means that most
of his reports of exempts are under the actual
number exempted.

General Walter drew a similar picture for

[1] *Ibid.*, p. 976.

Alabama.[1] The official figures for Alabama, 1,333, were much higher than for Mississippi in 1864, which showed that the Governor had exacted his pound of flesh in 1863, as it took several months to get these figures.[2] As in the case of Mississippi, the numbers reported were meaningless, for the governor in 1864 claimed every civil and military officer in the state, from the police in Selma to the governor in Montgomery,[3] making several thousands rather than a few hundred.

Governor Smith, of Virginia, remained friendly to the Confederate policy, but not so his legislature. That body by 1864 insisted that every officer named in the constitution and laws of the state was essential to the dignity and sovereignty—and we might add, happiness—of the state.[4] Smith delivered the legislature an indignant lecture for having exempted the great host of state and county officers named in the constitution and laws of the state, especially the 2,000 magistrates whose counties were within the enemies' lines, thus rendering them without official

[1] O. R., Ser. 4, Vol. III, p. 976.
[2] Ibid., pp. 851, 1102.
[3] Ibid., pp. 817, 818, 820, 849.
[4] Ibid., pp. 905-14.

duties.[1] The total number of officers thus exempted is not shown on the records, but we gather an idea that there were several thousand from the fact that there were, as already stated, 2,000 justices of the peace from the invaded counties alone. Governor Smith said that the officers from these counties were enough by themselves "to turn the tide of a great battle."[2]

Up until the late fall of 1864 South Carolina had asserted no claims over her state officers when the Confederate government required them for military service. As Governor Bonham wrote Governor Vance September 28, 1864, no persons were "reserved to the state, but all have gone into the Confederate service, from the classes of militia officers, magistrates, deputy clerks, and deputy sheriffs" on up to the highest officers of the state.[3] But even when Bonham wrote this letter to Vance South Carolina was reaching the breaking-point, and in December the legislature virtually repudiated all obligations to the Confederate government. This legislature nullified the slave impressment act of the Confederate government and then passed an ex-

[1] *Ibid.*   [2] *Ibid.*, p. 906.   [3] *Ibid.*, pp. 692-93.

emption act that, according to General Preston of the Bureau of Conscription, would have "the effect to nullify the existing law of Congress and forestall any further legislation of Congress looking to citizens of South Carolina for an increase of the army."[1] At one stroke South Carolina went to the front ranks of the opposition.

In order to understand just where South Carolina stood, it will benefit us to examine the provisions of this law. The governor could claim the exemption from Confederate military service of the members of the legislature, all judges of courts of law and equity, attorney- and solicitor-generals, secretaries of state, comptroller-general, state auditor and two assistants, treasurers of the upper and lower divisions, adjutant and inspector general and one assistant, quartermaster general, commissary general, state engineer and one assistant, aides-de-camp to the governor for each brigade, private secretary for the governor and his clerks, sheriffs and clerks of the courts, registers and commissioners in equity, tax collectors, cashiers, bookkeepers, and one teller of the state bank and each of its

[1] O. R., Ser. 4, Vol. III, p. 979.

branches, cadets of the military academy, teachers in South Carolina College, superintendent, physicians, and keepers of the lunatic asylum, members of the Board of Relief of Soldiers' Families, the president, cashier, bookkeepers, and one teller for each bank and savings institution, deputy sheriffs, one editor for each newspaper and such pressmen and printers as the editor might need, all members of police and fire departments at Columbia and Charleston, all employees in factories and public works belonging to the state, all college teachers, and any number of white persons the governor might think necessary for policing the country.[1] The Governor executed this law to the letter.[2] During the last few months of the Confederacy, when the state-rights reaction held sway, the Governor probably exempted several thousand able-bodied men from military service.

The records do not tell us all about Texas, but we will remember that in our study of local defense the legislature claimed all conscripts not in Confederate service at the time, and that Murrah detailed 5,000 men to haul cotton for

[1] *Ibid.*, pp. 979–80.   [2] *Ibid.*, pp. 1004–5.

the state.[1] Again, we will remember that General Greer complained to the Confederate authorities that every officer, down to the lowest deputies and subdeputies, were exempted by the state judges through the writ of habeas corpus.[2]

But, as in some other state-rights claims, North Carolina was easily first in the number of so-called state officers exempted. Vance had kept as many men for local defense as possible and he did likewise in the matter of state and militia officers. He had asserted this claim soon after coming into office, laying claim to the pettiest officials imaginable as being necessary for the efficient governing of the state.[3] By 1864 Vance was making a much wider claim to exemptions: when the Confederate government attempted to withdraw the details from the forty North Carolina factories working for Vance, or refused to grant new details in order to force these factories to turn over part of their output to the Confederacy, he coolly claimed every operative he needed on the ground that he was

[1] See chapter on "Local Defense," pp. 60–61.

[2] See chapter on "Suspension of the Writ of Habeas Corpus," pp. 195–98.

[3] O. R., Ser. 4, Vol. II, pp. 464–65, 466, 632–33.

a state officer. Vance boldly announced to the Confederate authorities that beside the state officers heretofore claimed, he claimed "any and all persons in the actual employ of the state in any department where the law enjoins duties to be done which require the employment of such persons."[1] Shortly after this, Preston, of the conscript bureau, reported that the Governor had exempted "all persons employed in any form by the state . . . . such as workmen in factories, salt markets, etc.," and that the bureau no longer had the power to enforce the law "in opposition to the Governor's certificate or claims."[2]

As in the case of Governor Brown and Governor Clark, Vance did not consider an official certificate necessary to exempt a person—the proclamation or the state law covering the class in which the man fell was deemed sufficient. The Supreme Court of North Carolina, as has been seen in the case of *Johnson* v. *Mallet*, upheld Vance's position,[3] and the result was that the rec-

[1] *Ibid.*, Vol. III, pp. 754–55; see also chapter on "Relation of the States to their Troops in the Confederate Service," pp. 124–25.

[2] O. R., Ser. 4, Vol. III, p. 867; cf. *ibid.*, pp. 850–51.

[3] *Ibid.*, pp. 754–55; see also above, p. 125.

ords show only part of the number actually exempted. The actual numbers given are startling; if they had been sent to operate on Sherman's line of communication at this time he might have found Atlanta a prison instead of a prize. On January 25, 1864, Lieutenant Colonel E. D. Blake, on special inspection service, submitted a report in which he credits North Carolina with 25,000 "exempted by claim of the governor."[1] On November 23, 1864, Preston made a report "of the number of state officers exempted in each state on the certificates of the governors of each state," in which he credited North Carolina with 14,675;[2] but, as we have seen, the Governor was not granting certificates to all exempted, so that the number of exempts was larger than the number of certificates. Later on, when Preston had been thoroughly lambasted by President Davis and the existence of the bureau threatened by military conscription on account of the large number of exempts, he contended that the enrolling officer, Peter Mallet, had made a gross error, and that the number was much less than indicated

[1] O. R., Ser. 4, Vol. III, p. 98.

[2] *Ibid.*, pp. 850–51.

in the report.[1] But we must not overlook the fact that the Bureau of Conscription was on trial for its life and that there was a deadly feud between it and the "army" which demanded "military conscription" instead of the lax civil methods heretofore used. Bragg, Pillow, Johnston, and Kemper represented the army group who contended for military conscription as already used for a short time by Pillow in Alabama, Mississippi, and Tennessee, and they were doing all in their power to discredit Preston and he in turn was doing all in his power to make a good showing for himself and his Bureau.[2] With this quarrel between the Bureau and army in mind, we should naturally expect Preston to welcome any opportunity to make a reduction in the numbers carried on his exemption reports, so that the figures of Blake—25,000—were probably nearer the truth than those of the conscription chief.

The facts presented in this short summary give some slight idea as to the material damage

[1] *Ibid.*, p. 867. Mallet finally agreed that 8,000 was nearer the number when Preston had induced him to see the error of his way.

[2] For illustrations of this contest, see: O. R., Ser. 4, Vol. III, pp. 568, 609, 618–21, 624–25, 640–41, 675, 732, 738, 854–56, 859–63, 1176, 1177.

done by state opposition to the conscription laws.[1] Preston, who could tell the truth when not attacked by the "army," said in a report of March, 1864, that during his term of office "there has never been one man sent to the field by the state authority. The collisions between the state and the conscript authorities have been universally caused by the effort of the state to keep the men from the conscript officers. . . . . From one end of the Confederacy to the other, every constituted authority, every officer, every man, and woman, is engaged in opposing the enrolling officer in the execution of his duties."[2]

[1] It must be pointed out, in case the fact is not obvious that there is a part duplication in the personnel of the exempted state and militia officers and that of the "local-defense" troops. For instance, all the militia officers, and in some states many of the minor state officers, belonged to the state forces. This, of course, keeps the number below what otherwise might seem an absurd figure.

[2] O. R., Ser. 4, Vol. III, p. 225.

CHAPTER V

IMPRESSMENT OF PROPERTY

When the Confederate currency began to depreciate and prices began to rise correspondingly, it became difficult for the commissary department to obtain supplies. This was because the farmer, on account of constantly rising prices, preferred to hold his produce just as long as his financial condition would permit, or at least until his goods should begin to spoil. In short, the rising market made a speculator of every farmer, producer, or capitalist. Another reason which made the producer hold his goods was that he did not care to hold the Confederate currency, since it would probably depreciate further and finally might become worthless on his hands. An additional motive for not selling at market prices to the Confederate commissary—especially in the last year of the war—was the belief that the Confederate government, which purchased on a credit, would not be able to honor even in Confederate currency the debts thus made.

This situation alone would have necessitated impressment of supplies for the army, but there was a common feeling shared by both government and people that the producers and speculators were taking unfair advantage of the general distress by their high prices. So high indeed were the prices charged for supplies that the government felt that even though the farmer were willing to part with his goods it would soon plunge the Confederacy into bankruptcy to pay the market prices. A double motive, then, existed for the policy of impressment soon adopted: the necessity of forcing the farmers and merchants to release their goods, and the necessity of purchasing at a low price fixed by the government.[1] Until 1863 there was no law on the statute book that legalized the practice, and the Confederate authorities were compelled to act upon custom and general principle. It was not long until a great deal of opposition developed at this rather broad assumption of power and the too often arbitrary methods employed.[2]

[1] O. R., Ser. 4, Vol. III, pp. 594–97; Schwab, *Confederate States*, p. 202; cf. O. R., Ser. 4, Vol. II, pp. 26, 39, 235, 441, 442, for instances.

[2] Jones, *Diary*, I, 194, 198; *Journal of the Confederate Congress*, I, 761; *ibid.*, III, 37; O. R., Ser. 4, Vol. I, pp. 646, 666; *ibid.*, Vol. III, pp. 26, 39, 235, 441, 442.

IMPRESSMENT OF PROPERTY

The clamor reached the ears of Congress and the state-rights and anti-administration group immediately challenged the President to show his authority for the exercise of such power. William Simms, of Kentucky, introduced a resolution in the Senate on January 19, 1863, "that the president be requested to communicate to the senate . . . . whether the military authorities . . . . have been authorized to seize and impress for public use flour and other articles of value, the property of private citizens of the Confederate States."[1] Immediately afterward he submitted another, aimed at the growing military despotism at Richmond. It said:

> The right of the protection of life, liberty, and property is the right inviolable of every citizen of the Confederate States, and the right is made sacred by the highest guarantees of the Constitution, and neither Congress nor the executive officers . . . . of this government have power in any manner or under any pretense whatsoever to impair, interfere with, or destroy this inherent or inviolable right, ... that all seizures or impressment of any such property are in violation of the plainest provisions of the Constitution, are destructive of the most sacred rights of the citizens, and are an unwarranted breach of the plighted faith of the government to the citizens thereof and are therefore void.[2]

[1] *Journal of the Confederate Congress*, III, 20.   [2] *Ibid.*, p. 21.

As a result of these protests and of an obvious necessity Congress passed a law authorizing and regulating impressment of private property for public use,[1] which was approved by the President March 26, 1863.[2] This law provided that the commissary and quartermaster officers, whose duties were to furnish any supplies or other property necessary for the army, should make all impressments. These officers were first authorized to make an offer to the owner of the property, and in case of failure to agree, the officer and owner were to appoint, each, a disinterested and loyal citizen as judge. If the impressment officer did not agree to the price fixed by this committee of disinterested citizens, he could then appeal the case to the state impressment commissioners whose decision would be final. This state commission, one member appointed by the governor and one by the president, though acting as a court of last resort, also was engaged in studying the market conditions

[1] *Journal of the Confederate Congress*, III, 37, 38, 47, 50, 56, 72, 90, 102–5, 112, 122–34, 142–45, 147, 148, 173, 189–91, 194, 209, 216; *ibid.*, VI, 22, 23, 61, 62, 72, 83, 95, 100–2, 105–7, 178, 179, 186, 216–18, 255.

[2] *Ibid.*, III, 216; *ibid.*, VI, 255; O. R., Ser. 4, Vol. II, pp. 469–72; Schwab, p. 202.

in various localities and fixing the maximum prices which the local impressment agents might offer for goods. The law provided that only the surplus might be impressed and that a sufficient quantity must always be left for the owner's family, his slaves, and stock. A receipt must always be given by the officer showing his organization, time and place of impressment, and amount paid. In case actual payment was not made at the time, the certificate was to be good for the money when presented to the proper disbursing officer.

Finally, the act provided for the impressment of slaves; but in this case the impressment was to be made "according to the rules and regulations provided in the laws of the state wherein they are impressed." In case no state law existed, the Secretary of War was to make rules in accordance with the section of the impressment law relating to the accumulation of general supplies.

The central principle to this act—taking property and paying prices set by the government—remained in force, only slight amend-

223

ments being made[1] until the fall and winter of 1864–65, when it broke down under the attack of its opponents and natural causes. It may be added that a supplementary law for the impressment of slaves was passed February 17, 1864— probably due to the extreme difficulty found in obtaining slaves under the regular impressment act. This law specified 20,000 as the number to be impressed at any one time, and provided that the method of impressment should be the same as in the law of March 26, 1863.[2]

Impressment, as we have seen, before it was regulated by these laws, raised a clamor; but conditions had not reached the point before March, 1863, where impressment was universally necessary in order to procure supplies, and the outcry was not so great. But after the Vicksburg and Gettysburg campaign of 1863 the credit and currency of the Confederate States depreciated rapidly, making impressment the only possible method of wringing the supplies and negroes from the reluctant planters, and soon a universal

[1] *Journal of the Confederate Congress*, VI, 457, 863; Schwab, *Confederate States*, p. 202, footnote 2.

[2] O. R., Ser. 4, Vol. III, p. 208.

cry of wrath and distress arose. One of the leading newspapers, quoted by the *Annual Cyclopaedia* in 1863 as showing the state of public feeling and as representative of the attitude of the southern press, said: "These impressments have done more to shake the confidence of the country in the capacity of its public men in civil office . . . . than any other cause and all other causes combined."[1] Governor Watts said, January 19, 1864, "The impressment of private property is always odious. . . . . If we fail to achieve our independence in the contest, the failure will arise from breaking down the spirits of the people by acts of tyranny of our officers."[2]

While impressment was absolutely necessary in order to carry on the war, at the same time it helped to bring the war to a close. Without it the prosecution of the war would have collapsed immediately, and with it the war could not last indefinitely because of the bitterness aroused. It invaded one of the most sacred precincts of state rights—the right of property in goods and slaves.

[1] *Harper's Annual Cyclopaedia* (1863), p. 207.

[2] O. R., Ser. 4, Vol. III, p. 37.

One might very aptly say that the Confederacy had lighted the candle at both ends.

Before entering the controversy that forms the most important phases of this subject, let us state briefly the actual situation as far as possible. Due to the stress of circumstances, the lack of proper organization, constant emergencies, and other easily understood conditions, the regulation supply officers were often not available, and in order that the army might not suffer, regular line officers and even privates were frequently compelled to make the impressments in the face of the law which enjoined that this duty must be performed only by commissary and quartermaster officers. Technically, therefore, the certificates granted by these unauthorized agents were illegal, and in many parts of the country the populace had a great deal of difficulty in collecting their money from the disbursing officers. Frequently, too, thieves and robbers seized the property of helpless citizens and gave certificates which naturally were not honored by the authorities, and immediately the Confederacy was blamed with it all. Again, the impressment agents, due to lack of transportation facilities took the property of those who lived nearest the army camps and railroads. This resulted in unequal sharing of the burden—though the burden usually fell upon the big planters who were most able to bear it. Further, in violation of the law, horses were occasionally seized by cavalry bands to furnish remounts; and impressment officers had a way of pouncing upon goods in transit to the city markets, which caused the urban population to suffer. Again—and we will remember it was one of the purposes of the law —the impressment commissioners of the state fixed the prices which agents might pay far below the market price. Finally, and more burdensome still, the Confederate agents in the last year of the war, as has been suggested, were forced because of lack of funds to impress goods without paying the owner. They gave receipts which the Confederate government was unable to honor because of lack of funds. There were about $500,000,000 thus due for impressed goods by March, 1865.[1]

[1] For report of Confederate officials, see O. R., Ser. 1, Vol. LII, Part II, pp. 695–99; *ibid.*, XXXIV, Part II, pp. 933–34; *ibid.*, XLVI, Part II, pp. 1220, 1221; *ibid.*, Ser. 4, Vol. III, pp. 40, 594–95, 689, 1018, 1019, 1094.

STATE RIGHTS IN THE CONFEDERACY

CONTROVERSY OVER IMPRESSMENT

These bad features of the impressment system were freely acknowledged by the Confederate authorities; but, as they contended, they were evils arising from an "inexorable necessity." On the other hand, those who were hostile to the general policies of the central government accused the system of many other evils, and contended bitterly that impressment was not necessary but was another deliberate assumption of despotic powers. Stephens was the undoubted head of the opposition. Toombs and Yancey were the next strongest; then followed Governors Brown, of Georgia; Vance, of North Carolina; Lubbock, of Texas; Watts, of Alabama; and Allen, of Louisiana; and Senators Oldham, of Texas; Haynes and Simms, of Kentucky; and Herschel V. Johnson, of Georgia; and Congressmen Foote, of Tennessee; and Dortch, of North Carolina. These were the nucleus about which an ever increasing body was forming. They were so strongly attached to the idea of state sovereignty that rather than give up their theory they preferred to see the whole Confederacy go down in defeat. This sentiment was well expressed by

Yancey when he said "that it is far better for a free people to be vanquished in open combat with the invader than voluntarily to yield liberties and their constitutional safeguards to the stealthy progress of . . . . executive usurpation toward the establishment of a military dictatorship."[1] The struggle over impressment of property may be treated under three heads: impressment of (*a*) supplies; (*b*) negroes; (*c*) railroads.

a) IMPRESSMENT OF SUPPLIES

The Georgia group, Toombs, the Stephens brothers, Herschel V. Johnson, and Joe Brown, being the very backbone of the state-rights group, was perhaps the first to voice the discontent with impressment. Toombs, the Stephenses, and Brown were so closely connected politically and as friends that what one said had usually been mulled over by the other members of the group. One cannot read the letters that passed between these men during the days of the Confederacy without being struck by the solidarity of this group, based upon intimate friend-

[1] *Richmond Enquirer*, in the *Montgomery Mail*, November 9, 1862.

ship intensified by similar views of state rights and a common hatred and fear of Davis.[1] Keeping in mind this intimate relation in dealing with the state of Georgia, it will always be proper and even necessary to discuss the reaction of the whole group toward impressment or any other question, for Toombs and Brown and Linton Stephens were almost as much vice-presidents of the Confederate states as Alexander Stephens, while the two Stephens and Toombs were as much the governors of Georgia as Brown and at times more so.

The first tilt between Georgia and the Confederacy over impressment came in October, 1861. Brown refused to loan the military authorities the rolling stock of the Western and Atlanta Railroad, owned by Georgia.[2] After his refusal the central government ordered Major Ashe to impress the stock, and Brown, on getting ear of the order, took fire and wired Benjamin, Acting secretary of War, that he should "resist the impressment with military force if necessary."[3] Soon the pressure of war upon the northern

[1] *Toombs, Stephens, Cobb Correspondence*, pp, 528–62.
[2] O. R., Ser. 4, Vol. I, p. 646.   [3] *Ibid.*, p. 666.

borders of Georgia brought the attendant unauthorized seizures of property, and in February, 1863, Brown again made a violent protest
to Davis. He pointed out that owing to a
drought there had not been enough corn grown
to feed the population in Cherokee County, and
that the Confederate soldiers were seizing what
little had been made, and that the people were
threatened with starvation. He demanded that
President Davis give his immediate attention to
the abuse or there would be trouble.[1]

But the "inexorable necessity" for impressment continued, and Brown, as was his wont,
began throwing all kinds of impediments in the
way of the officers and agents of the Confederacy.[2] He became so exasperated finally that he
called the legislature together and with the aid
of the Stephenses and Toombs[3] had a law passed
making impressment by persons without proper
authority a felony punishable by flogging and
ten years' imprisonment, and resolutions de-

[1] *Ibid.*, Vol. II, p. 405; cf. *Confederate Records of Georgia*, II,
514-17.

[2] O. R., Ser. 4, Vol. II, p. 915; *Confederate Records of Georgia*, II,
473-76.

[3] *Annual Cyclopaedia* (1863), pp. 207-8.

231

manding that all impressment agents of conscript age be immediately removed and native
Georgians not of military age appointed.[1] Seddon protested that unless Georgia would withdraw all obstacles and give her whole-hearted co-
operation in gathering supplies for the army it
was very doubtful "whether the army of General
Bragg could be maintained."[2] Brown replied
that he was doing all he could to aid in obtaining
supplies by legal means, but that he was making
war on all other kinds. However, he was un-
alterably opposed to impressment as a means.
Some districts, he said, were absolutely stripped:
"Taking from the people all they have to subsist
upon, in violation of the law, denying them the
right given by law of arbitration," while other
districts were left unmolested, and the burden,
consequently, laid unequally upon the shoulders
of the people. Finally, he contended, if the Confederate government would give just compensation—the market price—impressment would not
be necessary in order to collect supplies for the
army.[3]

[1] *Confederate Records of Georgia*, II, 514–17; Schwab, *Confederate States*, p. 205; O.R., Ser. 4, Vol. II, pp. 944, 988.

[2] *Ibid.*, p. 915. [3] O. R., Ser. 4, Vol. II, p. 944; Jones, *Diary*, II, 99.

IMPRESSMENT OF PROPERTY

It was at this time that Robert Toombs again stepped heavily upon the political stage of Georgia and began his opposition to the Confederate policies. Before entering into his fight against the administration, let us pause a moment and review the last two years of his public career up until this moment when he entered Georgia politics. Toombs, who had been one of the first men of the South before the Civil War, was grievously disappointed when he was not made the first president of the Confederacy. He considered himself the best-qualified person for this position, and there were those who agreed with Toombs in his estimate of himself. So after his failure to obtain the Confederate presidency it was galling to this individualistic southerner to have to accept a subordinate position under Davis, whom he already hated as his successful rival. After a short term in Davis' cabinet he found it more than he could endure to submit to the dictation of the President in matters in which he considered himself more competent than his chief. He then resigned and turned to the army, only to find himself a mere political general subordinated to men who were Davis'

appointees and "janissaries," as he was pleased
to call them. His experience was even more bitter and disappointing in the army than it had
been in the cabinet of his rival. Here absolutely
no attention was paid to his officious efforts to
instruct the military leaders of the "old army,"
as he called them, as to the proper strategy to
adopt. Scant courtesy was paid him by the
"West Point gang,"[1] and after a few months he
became convinced that Davis and the "old
army" group were purposely undermining his
military career and attempting his ruin. In this
state of mind it was not hard for him to come to
the belief that the President was a scheming
tyrant, grasping at absolute power through his
control of the army. The Confederacy was really
not big enough for both Toombs and Davis, so
it seems. At last, in 1863, his cup of bitterness
was overflowing and he decided to resign his
commission in the army. However, as he was
absolutely sure that "that scoundrel, Jeff Davis"
would "avail himself of any opportunity" to
drive him from the army in dishonor,[2] Toombs

[1] Another one of his phrases. Like many other political generals,
Toombs had a deadly antipathy for the officers of West-Point origin.

[2] *Toombs, Stephens, Cobb Correspondence*, p. 608.

waited until he could resign on his own volition. As soon as he had secured the acceptance of his resignation from "so false and hypocritical a wretch" as Davis,[1] he bade farewell to his troops and turned his steps toward Georgia. From here he wrote W. W. Burwell, of Virginia: "As to opposition, I do not see how anything else is left to me or anybody else except the entire surrender of the country, executive, legislative, and judicial departments, to Mr. Davis."[2] Nor did Toombs fail to live up to this self-appointed task. It was unfortunate for the Confederacy that he did not remain in the army where his political talent could have less play. On his return to Georgia he immediately launched an attack upon the financial policy of the government in an article published in the *Constitutionalist* and copied widely throughout the country;[3] and in November, 1863, we thus find him aiding Brown in his successful efforts to pass laws obstructive to impressment through the Georgia legislature. His speech before the assembly was

[1] Toombs' words (*Tooms, Stephens, Cobb Correspondence*, p. 611).

[2] *Ibid.*, p. 629; Mrs. Chestnut, *A Diary from Dixie*, p. 171.

[3] *Toombs, Stephens, Cobb Correspondence*, pp. 622–27; cf. Jones, *Diary*, II, 39.

a bitter attack upon impressment and its sponsors. Such methods of obtaining supplies he denounced as despotic and tyrannical, placing the burden of the war unequally upon the shoulders of the people, destroying personal liberty and freedom, and violating the fundamental principles of the Constitution. When things had reached such a pass, all, he said, must be lost. Congress had "made a fatal blunder" in stamping its approval upon the policy which had "sown the seeds of discontent broadcast over the land, and is generating hostility to the government itself." Like Brown and other opponents of impressment, Toombs contended that the necessity of such would be obviated by paying the market price for goods.[1]

Herschel V. Johnson raised his voice also in protest against impressment. On August 16, 1864, he wrote Secretary of the Treasury Trenholme that the impressment law, as it was being enforced, was violating the Constitution very seriously. The government, he admitted, had the power to impress property, but the "power

[1] *Annual Cyclopaedia* (1863), pp. 207–8. For account of Toombs' life, see Phillips, *Life of Toombs*.

of impressment does not carry with it the power to regulate prices." The impressing agents "must give just compensation." This regulation of price was one objection, but another even more serious, he said, was that it could not be universal; every citizen could not be subjected to it, and of necessity it was applied to those unfortunate farmers whose plantations were near the railroads or other lines of transportation. The spirit, if not the letter, of the Constitution required that "all should bear alike the burden of the war," and impressment could not thus be borne alike by all. Furthermore, he said, the government was not paying cash for the impressed goods, but was giving only a receipt, a promise to pay, "which promise may be redeemed in a reasonable time, or in a year, or never." His remedy was to levy unlimited tax, which would not have the unjust features of impressment since all would share alike in the burdens.[1] On September 5 Johnson wrote to Secretary of War Seddon expressing the same objections. He warned Seddon that the limit had been reached in Georgia, and that impressment could

[1] O. R., Ser. 4, Vol. III, pp. 594-97.

no longer be enforced. People were generally refusing to part with their goods at schedule prices "which offered $5 a bushel for wheat when it was selling in the open market at $15 to $25."[1]

Other men of less note added their voices to the swelling chorus of state rights that had been condemning the policy of impressment. December 24, 1864, P. A. Lawson wrote President Davis that the Confederate cavalry under Wheeler had been feeding upon the corn fields, and that the receipts for the corn had not been honored by the Confederate disbursing officers. He complained that Wheeler's cavalry had driven off the stock and hogs for miles on each side while retreating before Sherman, and that the Confederate government refused to accept the old-issue paper currency[2] in payment for the tithe or tax in kind which "Wheeler's robbers" had burnt or destroyed. He assured the President that the people of Georgia had about come to the point where they did not care which army

[1] O. R., Ser. 4, Vol. III, pp. 662–63.

[2] This currency had been withdrawn by law months before this time, but the people refused to exchange it for new currency, and the government finally refused to accept it in payment of tax.

won, as Sherman was not making war any harder for them than their own army.[1]

At length the Georgia supreme court came to the side of Brown and his party of state-righters. It rendered the decision that the Confederate authorities must pay a just compensation for all goods impressed, and just compensation was interpreted to mean whatever the local appraisers determined. Under ordinary circumstances the local appraisers always assessed the value of the impressed property at neighborhood rates, and the decision of the court simply meant that the Confederate government would be compelled to pay the local market price in Georgia.[2] From Texas and Louisiana came complaints of the unjust operation of the impressment laws,[3] and in Mississippi it was declared that impressment had degenerated into highway robbery.[4]

Illegal and unauthorized seizures, as else-

[1] O. R., Ser. 4, Vol. III, pp. 967–68; cf. Jones, *Diary*, II, 116.

[2] O. R., Ser. 1, Vol. XLVI, Part II, pp. 1214–16; Schwab, *Confederate States*, p. 689; Jones, *Diary*, II, 111.

[3] O. R., Ser. 1, Vol. XXXIV, Part II, pp. 865, 929, 933, 975.

[4] Schwab, *Confederate States*, p. 207; Jones, *Diary*, II, 56; O. R., Ser. 4, Vol. III, p. 689.

where, caused great dissatisfaction in Virginia.[1] But one of the most constant complaints was not of the lawless application of impressment, but of the unjustness of its lawful operation. Being so near the army, that state was practically stripped of all surplus supplies, only enough being left to support those from whom goods had been taken. This brought great suffering upon the people of Richmond and other cities, and upon the entire non-producing population of the country. The newspapers were inclined to lay the blame upon the farmers, whom they accused of holding their supplies, rather than upon the Confederate government. At length the farmers began to protest against being made the scapegoat. One planter in Louisa County wrote that the Confederate government had left nothing for them to sell to the cities. It had, he said, taken the entire surplus of wheat "at the fixed price of $5 a bushel, barely leaving sufficient for seed and family use," and that "all the hogs and oats had long since been hauled off to the army."[2] A James River farmer said that the government

[1] O. R., Ser. 4, Vol. III, p. 43.

[2] *Annual Cyclopaedia* (1863), p. 206.

had "impressed all the wheat and flour and beef in this region which was destined for Richmond."[1] At length the discontent became so general that the Virginia legislature passed resolutions condemning impressment[2] and Representative Goode introduced a resolution in Congress that the law should be so altered as to leave enough surplus for the relief of the non-producing population.[3]

In Alabama, the Confederate government met with opposition in the enforcement of impressment. The government agents sent out notices to the farmers not to sell or remove any of their surplus, but to hold it for government use,[4] and about the same time the commissioner for the state, John J. Walker undertook a census of supplies in order to know what Alabama might be depended upon to furnish. This prying into the closets and smokehouses was not at all pleasing to the people, especially since they had not been told what its object was. At length, after the Governor had made an angry inquiry as

[1] *Ibid.*   [2] Schwab, *Confederate States*, p. 207.

[3] *Journal of the Confederate Congress*, VI, 542; *Annual Cyclopaedia* (1863), pp. 229–30.

[4] *Montgomery Weekly Mail*, December 1, 1863.

to the object of Walker's census, the latter explained his purpose. Governor Watts accepted his explanation, but he reminded him that it should have been made long before while the people were being provoked by his agents.

Watts took occasion also to express his opinion of impressment in general. "It is," he said, "a better policy for the government to pay double prices than to make impressments . . . . the impressment of property only aggravates the price and creates opposition to the government and our cause. The practical operation of the impressment system has been disastrous . . . . many of the impressment officers care neither for God nor man."[1] The legislature soon took up the opposition of the Governor and passed resolutions condemning the policy of impressment.[2] The opposition became so strong that impressment finally broke down. Walker, on January 25, 1865, wrote Commissary General Northup that the people had lost all faith in the Confederate government and were refusing to surrender their property except for money.[3]

[1] O. R., Ser. 4, Vol. III, p. 37; Jones, *Diary*, I, 191.

[2] Schwab, *Confederate States*, p. 207.

[3] O. R., Ser. 1, Vol. XLVI, Part II, pp. 1220–21.

IMPRESSMENT OF PROPERTY

Even the patient and long-suffering Governor Milton opposed impressment. The commissary agent of Florida, as in the other states, had sent a notice to each farmer that he was bound by said notice to consider all surplus beeves, hogs, and bacon impressed, and that he must not sell or move them.[1] This, if literally enforced, would have the effect of paralyzing all trade, and of depriving the non-producing class of subsistence. In his message of November 23, 1863, Milton, in great wrath, attacked the policy and proceedings of the impressment agents. If the order to hold all surplus at the disposal of the Confederate government should be enforced, he asked, how could the families of soldiers, and refugees from the invaded districts, and the population of the cities be saved from starvation? This was outrageous, unconstitutional, a violation of state rights, and "may God forbid," he exclaimed, "that any citizen of Florida should ever be so base and cowardly as to yield willingly to any government or usurpation of power" the most sacred rights guaranteed by the Constitution "rather than meet death without fear in

[1] *Ibid.*, Ser. 4, Vol. II, p. 976.

their vindication." Better, he exhorted them, "that Florida should be a waste land of flowers enriched with the blood of her brave citizens than to be inhabited by them as slaves or willing to be slaves." He urged the legislature to enact a law quickly that would protect the rights of the citizens and bring those to justice who violated these rights.[1] As a result of this urgent appeal, the legislature passed a law dealing severely with any impressment agent who violated its provisions and overstepped his authority.[2]

As one might suppose, impressment was very unpopular in North Carolina, and Governor Vance by his continued opposition only added to its unpopularity. On December 21, 1863, he wrote Secretary Seddon a spiteful protest against the seizure of private property by the Confederate cavalry. He was sure the Department had no idea as to the extent and character of the impressments. He wrote:

It is enough in many places to breed a rebellion in a loyal country against the Confederacy, and has actually

[1] O. R., Ser. 4, Vol. II, p. 976.

[2] *Ibid.*, Vol. III, pp. 14-21. But trouble continued between the Confederate authorities and the Governor. He accused the Confederate agents of impressing milk-cows and leaving the people to starve (*ibid.*, pp. 45-48); cf. *ibid.*, p. 560.

been the cause of much alienation of feeling in many parts of North Carolina. . . . . If God Almighty had yet in store another plague worse than all others which he had intended to have let loose on the Egyptians in case Pharaoh still hardened his heart, I am sure it must have been a regiment or so of half-armed, half-disciplined Confederate cavalry. Had they been turned loose among Pharaoh's subjects with or without an impressment law he would have been so sensible of the anger of God that he never would have followed the children of Israel to the Red Sea. No sir! Not an inch! He wanted to know if a few could not be shot as a wholesome example to the rest of them. In case something was not done, he said, he would be forced to call out the militia and levy actual war against them.[1]

The legislature, responsive to such sentiment on the part of Vance, passed resolutions denouncing all the evils of impressment, demanding that the Confederate government "stop all such illegal proceedings." Finally the resolutions requested that the Governor use every honorable means to retain the remaining provisions in the state.[2] On January 4, 1864, Seddon replied to Vance's complaints. He pointed out that the law and all instructions and regulations

[1] *Ibid.*, Vol. II, pp. 1061–62; Jones, *Diary*, II, 119.

[2] O. R., Ser. 4, Vol. II, p. 1066; Schwab, *Confederate States*, pp. 206–7.

based upon it allowed the citizen from whom the goods had been impressed sufficient food to carry on his business, and that "much of the evil complained of is the result of inexorable necessity."[1] But Vance would not accept a mere explanation: he wanted something done. So on February 25 he wrote Seddon again, repeating his former complaints against impressment. He urged, as a partial remedy for illegal seizures, that all such losses on the part of North Carolina citizens should be credited to the current taxes they owed the Confederacy. He was sure this would quiet much disaffection and bring to the support of the government a "large class of persons who think and feel they are outside the pale of its protection."[2] Meanwhile, Vance had been carrying on a quarrel with Davis over the suspension of the writ of habeas corpus, peace proposals, and other matters,[3] and on February 9, having failed to obtain proper satisfaction from Seddon, he dragged the impressment troubles into this controversy. The system had become unbearable, he wrote Davis, "because intrusted to men

---

[1] O. R., Ser. 4, Vol. III, pp. 2–3.

[2] *Ibid.*, p. 177. [3] See chapter on habeas corpus, pp. 177–80.

246

unprincipled and filled to overflowing with the petty meanness of small minds dressed in a little brief authority." The files of his office were filled with complaints of outraged citizens whose grievances the Confederate government had refused to redress.[1]

The President demanded that Vance produce specific cases which had been ignored, as he claimed by the Confederate authorities. The Governor promptly answered that he had time and again sent up to the Secretary of War complaints of wrong and outrage and that not a single case had been redressed, and that others had been submitted to the generals in command of the Department, and "after going through the circumlocution of military references for weeks, perhaps for months, are finally 'respectfully returned to Governor Vance for his information'; that is to say, the matter stopped in the acceptance of the story of the accused party as a full exculpation from all accusations." A typical case was one that happened in Tyrrell County. The impressing officers, he said, had actually taken a man's team out from the plow, where-

[1] O. R., Ser. 1, Vol. LI, Part II, p. 819.

upon the farmers had put their means together and sent one, Lewis, to Richmond to obtain redress. But Lewis had only been lodged in Castle Thunder for his pains, upon the accusation of the very men who had seized his horses.[1] Davis replied that not one of these cases had ever been placed before him by the Governor, and the latter still had failed to forward him the papers necessary to redress the grievances. In the mind of the President it was a plain case of a governor's attempting to bring discredit upon the administration, rather than an honest effort to settle a difficulty. There is little doubt but that the President was correct. Impressment was odious, but the people would have borne it for a long time had Vance supported the Confederate government. As it was, the impressment system in North Carolina utterly failed in the fall of 1864, and the Confederate government was forced to pay cash for all it bought and to offer the top of the market.[2]

The summer and fall of 1863 were filled with protests against impressments in South Carolina.

[1] O. R., Ser. 1, Vol. LI, Part II, p. 832.

[2] *Ibid.*, Ser. 4, Vol. III, p. 932; *ibid.*, Ser. 1, Vol. XLVI, Part II, p. 1221.

On October 8 the legislature, voicing this discontent, passed resolutions condemning the system in no uncertain tone. Such a law, declared the resolutions, could be justified only by dire necessity, and under all circumstances should be enforced equitably and with discretion. But these considerations had been disregarded: impressment had been made at some convenient spot when the agents could have purchased supplies a short distance off if they had not been too lazy to make the effort. The result of this was that those who were convenient to the impressing officer had been stripped, while those farther off had gone free. But the most unjust of all, declared the resolutions, was that in many cases the supplies set apart by the farmers for the tax in kind or even stored in some dépôt had not been called for or moved, while the agents went ahead impressing in other neighborhoods nearby because they were too lazy to go any distance from their posts.[1] Governor Bonham submitted these resolutions to Secretary Seddon

[1] *Ibid.*, Ser. 4, Vol. II, p. 863. This was often the case, but its explanation lies in the lack of ability to obtain transportation off the main roads rather than in the "laziness" of impressing officers, as the resolutions put it.

in order that the latter might take some action against the abuses set forth. The Secretary replied on October 16 that all due consideration would be paid to the resolutions, but that it was a matter of regret that such complaints were "of so vague and general a character as to render it difficult to discover instances of offense or to administer a due corrective."[1] Complaints continued to pour into the Governor's office, so he again protested to the war department, submitting a batch of these complaints for the consideration of the Secretary. Seddon ordered an investigation and it was decided that the complaints were practically all unfounded; that "it is when the impressment agents detect and seize the stores of these speculators . . . . and those in the hands of illiberal farmers, ... that these complaints . . . . come teeming in."[2]

Meanwhile the South Carolina legislature again passed resolutions against impressment, requesting that the Governor and Attorney-General should publish a statement of the law and the rights of the people under it, and that

[1] O. R., Ser. 4, Vol. II, pp. 875–76.

[2] Ibid., Vol. III, pp. 402–3.

the Governor should urge the South Carolina
delegation in Congress to take action for arrest-
ing the evil immediately.[1] So Bonham once more
brought the matter before the Secretary of War.
He reiterated the complaint already made by the
legislature. He added further complaint against
the general notices sent out to the farmers to
hold their surplus subject to the orders of the
Confederate government. This, he said, had
caused great distress among the very poor, and
among refugees, and the non-producing population of the cities and towns. Finally, he submitted the sworn statements of J. Robertson and
C. Montague, two prominent citizens, that the
impressing agents had dealt unjustly and illegal-
ly with them. Robertson's statement was to the
effect that the impressing agent had taken,
against his protest, two old cows with calf, and
the Governor wrote Seddon that he had heard
of other similar cases. The statement of Montague was that he had bought supplies for himself and neighbors, and that the impressment
agent had refused to let him move them until he
had received affidavits from him and others for

[1] *Ibid.*, pp. 407–8.

whom he had made the purchase that the supplies were for domestic use and not for speculation. Montague had become angry and said that "Lincoln or the devil could not have devised any better means of breaking up this Confederacy," and that if these "wolves," the impressment agents, were suffered to harass the country in any such way, "an insurrection of the citizens is imminent." Montague further swore that the agent had been insolent and insulting in his language and general conduct.

The war department made a thorough investigation of the two cases and it throws a significant light over much of the complaint against impressment. It shows that much of the discontent rose from the irritation of the people over the inherent evils of impressment rather than from the violation of the law by the agents, and that much of the complaint was without reasonable foundation, coming only from a class of citizens getting their inspirations from officials like Vance and Brown, who wished to bring the Confederate government into disrepute with the people. But as to the investigations: The subagent, Captain Meyers, whom J. Robertson accused of impressing two cows with calf, made an affidavit in which he stated that the order to impress the cows had never been carried out, as represented by Robertson, but that the cows were still in the latter's possession. Furthermore, Meyers said that when he served the impressment notice Robertson had exhibited twenty cows or more, from which he selected one yearling, whereupon Robertson had objected and had offered him two cows instead, saying he preferred to part with them rather than the yearling. Meyers said he had objected to taking the cows because they were with calf, but Robertson would not hear to any other selection. He suggested to the war department that Robertson had no other motive in his action than to create a ground for complaint and stir up discontent against the Confederate government.

Montague's complaint against the impressment agent was investigated by one Captain Means, who made a sworn statement as to the facts in the case. He said the whole trouble was that Montague was swelled up with his own importance and had become offended when the impressing agent asked for proofs that the goods he had purchased were for the use of himself and neighbors and not for speculation. He pointed out that the Confederate agent was only performing his duty in thus questioning Montague, as he knew the latter from nobody else. He said that Montague, on having his word questioned, had become enraged and had denounced and insulted the officer, who had returned it in kind. "It is by no means impossible," concluded Captain Mean's statement, "to provoke a man to say harsh things and then make an *ex parte* statement apparently injurious to him. This has been very often done against that much-abused class of men known as government agents, or as Mr. Montague would say, 'wolves.'"[1]

In several of the states, besides the controversy over general impressment of supplies and forage, there was much friction between the Confederate and state governments over the impressment of slaves and of railroad iron.

b) IMPRESSMENT OF SLAVES

In North Carolina the railroads on the coast were in constant danger of capture or destruc-

[1] For Governor Bonham's letter and inclosures of complaints from Robertson, Montague, and others, and the war department's investigation, see O. R., Ser. 4, Vol. III, pp. 402–15.

tion after 1862, which rendered the transportation of the Confederate supplies to Virginia precarious and uncertain. In order to put transportation of supplies and troops on a safer basis, the Confederate government finally determined to connect Danville, Virginia, and Greensboro, North Carolina, by an interior line that would be out of striking distance of the enemy. So about the middle of December, 1863, Seddon made a requisition upon Governor Vance for a number of slaves to construct the road through North Carolina, but the Governor refused to furnish the slaves.[1] About two months later the Secretary again urged the matter upon Vance. "Due to the danger to transportation on the coast," he said, this connection "was almost indispensable" to Confederate success in Virginia.[2] But Vance was determined. He refused again to furnish the slaves to help build the road. He recognized the importance, he said, of having an interior route to Virginia, but when all the circumstances were considered he did not feel justified in supplying the labor. In the first

[1] *Ibid.*, Vol. II, pp. 385-86.
[2] *Ibid.*

place, the planters in the east had been furnishing labor upon all the fortifications from Wilmington to Petersburg, and he did not feel that he should call upon these men for any further sacrifices in the matter of slaves. It hurt him, he concluded, to "refuse to do anything whatsoever which is requested by the Confederate authorities."[1] One might well smile at this last statement if he remembers just how accommodating the Governor had been in allowing the Confederate government to share in the output of his forty cotton and woolen factories, and in his large export and import business as well as many other things.

In refusing the requisition for slaves Vance was voicing the rapidly growing hostility of the North Carolina farmers to the Confederacy's using their slaves. The slaves often escaped or died or were disabled while in Confederate employ, and more often the government was unable to pay for their use promptly. In the fall of 1864 the legislature passed resolutions protesting against the further impressments of slaves, and against the "cruel and inhuman manner" in

[1] O. R., Ser. 4, Vol. II, pp. 393–94.

which they claimed the Confederate officers treated the slaves working for the government. Finally the legislature instructed Vance to lay the complaints before the Confederate authorities and demand that the abuses be stopped.[1] So on December 16 the Governor wrote President Davis a letter, stating the slave-impressment grievances, and demanding, in his usual manner, their prompt redress.[2]

The hostility to the impressment of slaves in South Carolina finally brought that state into an attitude of virtual nullification. The loss of impressed slaves by exposure and escape had produced such a state of mind among the planters that they sent men to the legislature with instructions to pass laws to prevent the impressment of their slaves by the Confederate government,[3] and on December 23, 1864, the legislature enacted a law that fulfilled the desire of these discontented planters. While it did not flatly nullify the Confederate laws for the impressment of slaves, its effect would be the same as though it had resorted to nullification. The Confederate

[1] *Ibid.*, Vol. III, pp. 945–46.

[2] *Ibid.*   [3] *Ibid.*, pp. 1018–19, 1020–23.

law of February, 1864, under which most of the impressments of slaves were at that time being made, provided for the impressment of 20,000, to work at any place within the Confederacy under the authority of the Confederate government for a period of twelve months. On the other hand, the South Carolina law in question provided that no slave should go out of the state, and that he could be withdrawn every four months and a new slave substituted, and that the state should retain authority over him. Finally, one-tenth of the male slave population between eighteen and forty-five could be impressed at one time.[1]

The effect of this law would be that the state would leave few slaves for the confederate government to impress; and if it had left them, since the Confederate law provided that all impressment should be made in accordance with the state law, the impressment, under the state law, would have left the slaves in the hands of the state, subject to use only within the limits of the state. Preston, who was in charge of the impressment of slaves, wrote Seddon that the law

[1] O. R., Ser. 4, Vol. III, pp. 963–64.

was intended, and would have the "effect, to prevent the accession of one slave to the Confederate service as a contribution to the public defense." It was a matter of pain to him, he said, that South Carolina, his native state, was the first to commit treason against the Confederacy in the form of law. The example would soon be followed by North Carolina and Georgia, "the executives of those states already having assumed the position." Alabama and Mississippi would then follow, and every state would be for itself. In fact, he lamented, it had about come to that pass anyway, with Governor Brown and Governor Vance and the legislature of South Carolina hostile to the Confederacy, and looking only to the interest of their own states.[1] Preston, finding it impossible to come to any kind of terms with South Carolina, from Richmond, finally made a journey into that state to arrange some kind of *modus vivendi*. But he obtained no concessions from the obdurate authorities. On January 15 he wrote Seddon that a regiment of cavalry with a pack of bloodhounds would be unable to obtain the slaves unless the state co-

[1] *Ibid.*, p. 979.

operated, and that he could not get any promise of co-operation from the Governor and the other authorities, so the situation was hopeless.[1]

Florida followed the example of South Carolina in the fall of 1864. The legislature, on December 7, passed a law which forbade the impressment of slaves by any except state authorities. In part, the law provided "that no impressment of slaves . . . . shall be made except in conformity with the provisions of this law, and if any shall be made in violation thereof it is hereby declared unlawful and void."[2] Florida had enrolled her name alongside the opposition, and no more slaves were to leave her borders for the general service.

The greatest sufferer, perhaps, from the impressment of slaves was the state of Virginia, for there were seldom less than 10,000 at work on the fortifications and railroads,[3] quite a number of whom were permanently disabled, escaped, or died. So, as in South Carolina, the planters elected a legislature which would protect their

[1] O. R., Ser. 4, Vol. III, pp. 1018–19; cf. *ibid.*, pp. 1058–59.

[2] *Ibid.*, p. 905.

[3] Jones, *Diary*, I, 183, 237; *ibid.*, II, 36, 37; cf. O. R., Ser. 4, Vol. III, p. 40.

interests. As a result, Virginia's law, if the Confederate authorities had impressed slaves in accordance with its terms as the Confederate law had provided, would have defeated the impressment to a very great extent. But the military necessity and the presence in Virginia of the Confederate government caused the authorities of the latter government to take matters in their own hands and impress whatever slaves they needed to throw up breastworks and build fortifications. Finally, in the early part of 1864, the legislature passed resolutions protesting against the impressment of negroes, and begging that the Confederate government make no further demands.[1] On February 20 Seddon replied that he regretted very much not to be able to defer to the wishes of so august a body, but that the safety of Richmond depended upon the use of slaves in erecting fortifications. Besides, he said, February was the best time their slaves could be spared from the farm.[2]

So the Confederate government continued to levy impressments upon the people. At length Congressman Baldwin, of Virginia, championed

[1] *Ibid.*, p. 162.   [2] *Ibid.*

the complaint of his state against the further impressment of slaves. He wrote Seddon, on July 20, expressing a doubt whether any of the impressments made heretofore by the Confederacy "except according to the state law and through the Governor and county courts" had been legal. In short, he questioned the legality of the whole Confederate impressment procedure in Virginia.[1] The next day Seddon replied that he was making the impressments under the Confederate laws. These laws had provided that impressment of slaves should be in accordance with the laws of the state, but he said, in case the laws of the state were not "coextensive with the necessity to be met," it would defeat the terms of the Confederate law to conform to the state legislation. No law, he said, was intended to defeat its own operation, so he had not made use of the Virginia statutes on impressment.[2] In September the necessity of the Confederate army became so great that the authorities impressed 5,000 additional slaves and ordered that all slaves found on the streets should be picked up.[3] This aroused

[1] O. R., Ser. 4, Vol. III, p. 547.   [2] Ibid., pp. 563–64.

[3] Ibid., Ser. 1, Vol. XLII, Part II, p. 1268; Jones, Diary, II, 300.

a storm of opposition so great that the House of Representatives of the Confederate Congress undertook an investigation. It passed a resolution calling upon the President to show his authority "for conducting an impressment of slaves in Virginia without regard to the state law on that subject."[1] On November 28 Seddon replied to the congressional inquiry, which Davis had placed on his hands. In the first place, he said, while the Confederate law proposed that the impressment of slaves should be according to state law, it did not require it in all cases. He pointed out that the law of February 16, 1864, gave authority by implication for generals in the field to impress slaves in cases of urgent necessity. The occasion of the impressment referred to by the congressional resolution was, he said, one of extreme necessity and the levy of slave labor was justifiable under the law referred to. In the second place, he said, if the law of February 16, 1864, were not sufficient authority, there was the law of March 26, 1863, for general impressment of property. Any property might be taken under the terms of this law "for the good

[1] O. R., Ser. 4, Vol. III, p. 851; Jones, *Diary*, II, 334.

of the service," and as negroes were property, their impressment fell under the operation of this law. In the third place, as he had already pointed out to Baldwin, since the Virginia law was inadequate and would defeat the intentions of the Confederate law if impressments were made in accordance with the state provisions, that section of the Confederate law that proposed to make use of the impressment machinery of the state had been disregarded—since no law was intended to defeat itself.[1]

There was similar trouble in other southern states over the impressment of slaves, especially in Alabama and Texas.[2]

The fear that the United States would ultimately interfere with slavery had disrupted the Union, and now the Confederacy was reaching out into the different states and literally upsetting the institution. The government was truly walking upon dangerous ground. Senator Wigfall related an incident that well illustrated this fact. He was on the train, he said, and saw a

[1] O. R., Ser. 4, Vol. III, pp. 851-53.

[2] Freemantle, *Three Months in the Southern States*, p. 159; cf. Mrs. Chestnut, *A Diary from Dixie*, p. 180.

woe-begone negro. He inquired of the negro as to the cause of his dejection, and the negro replied that he had left his master in great distress and that he was sad over that. The Senator asked what his master was sad about, and the negro replied that it was because the government had impressed his slave. His master, he said, had five sons who had been taken into the army, but he never had grieved over them; that it was only after the government had taken one of his slaves that he showed signs of being downhearted. "The patriotic planters," concluded Wigfall, "would willingly put their own flesh and blood into the army, but when you ask them for a negro, the matter approaches the point of drawing an eyetooth."[1]

c) IMPRESSMENT OF RAILROAD IRON

Evidently the impressment of railroad iron[2] caused some friction between the state and Confederate governments. Secretary Seddon, in his report to President Davis on November 4, 1864, intimated as much. He said that although the

---

[1] *Annual Cyclopaedia* (1863), pp. 231-32.

[2] The iron on one road was used to repair other more important roads.

necessity was manifest and was acknowledged by all, it was "rare the proprietors of the special roads whose property is thus sought to be appropriated are prepared to acquiesce in its selection for the sacrifice. Each local corporation finds abundant reason for further delay or special exemption in its own case," and interposes all possible legal obstructions to seizure by impressment. He said that almost invariably the corporation found a way of obtaining an injunction against the removal of iron pending the proverbially long proceedings of the suit in chancery. Not only that, but the state authorities had interceded "to thwart and delay action," with the result that "more than once the gravest consequences to the Confederacy had been risked by inability at the juncture to overcome such impediments and command the required rails."[1]

There were two outstanding cases of the kind referred to by Seddon in Alabama and Florida. The trouble in Alabama was over the property of the Alabama and Florida Railroad. The Confederate authorities, after a vain attempt to

[1] O. R., Ser. 4, Vol. III, pp. 767–68.

purchase the rails needed to connect certain points, finally impressed them. Immediately the authorities of the road sought to obtain an injunction to restrain the removal of the iron on the ground that the property being mortgaged, the impressment of the rails would impair the obligation of the contract. The matter was finally carried up to the supreme court of Alabama, where the right of making such impressment was sustained.[1] But the delay had cost the Confederacy much. With this experience in mind, Lieutenant Colonel Meriwether wrote, when the Confederate government was contemplating the removal of iron from three branch roads in order to connect Blue Mountain and Jacksonville: "The attempt to remove any of the three branches will probably be enjoined . . . . in which event we must await the process of dissolving it before the courts or take it by military force."[2]

The controversy in Florida lasted through

[1] *Alabama and Florida Railroad Company* v. *Kenney*, 39, Alabama, 307, cited in *Studies in Southern History and Politics*, pp. 128–29, by S.D. Brummer, in his article, "Judicial Interpretation of the Confederate Constitution."

[2] O. R., Ser. 4, Vol. III, pp. 742–43.

most of the Civil War, and well illustrates the method used to thwart the Confederate government in its efforts to obtain railroad iron. On March 10, 1862, the Confederate authorities issued orders to remove the rails on the road connecting Fernandina and Cedar Keys. The president of the road, Mr. Yulee, objected to its removal, but the orders for its removal were under execution in a few days after being issued, in spite of his objection.[1] But some time after this the railroad officials obtained an injunction and stopped the removal of the rails.[2] Finally the government, after being delayed about two years, proposed to take matters into its own hands and disregard the injunction, whereupon Governor Milton championed the cause of the railroad and demanded that the Confederate government have its officers obey the injunctions.[3] On July 28, 1864, Secretary Seddon replied to Milton's demand. He reminded the Governor of the obstructions thrown in the way of the removal of iron in Florida and elsewhere. "One would think," he said, "that honor, patri-

[1] O. R., Ser. 4, Vol. II, pp. 648–51.

[2] *Ibid.*, Vol. III, p. 561.   [3] *Ibid.*, p. 560.

otism, and public spirit would dictate a proffer to the country of property of the kind in such an emergency, and that shame would prevent the use of any obstructive measures against an object so necessary to public safety." But the Department, he said, had not had its expectations fulfilled. "Injunctions and other forms of delay have been resorted to in order to prevent its action under the act of Congress in such cases." He protested that the state courts had no authority to issue injunctions restraining Confederate officials from performing their duty under the law. The right to sue Confederate officers for misconduct was recognized, "but their official functions were not supposed to be subject to the jurisdiction or the control of the state authorities." The consequence of such state interposition, he said, would be fatal if persisted in to its logical conclusion. The generals in the field could be enjoined from pitching camp on private property, the tax collector could be restrained from collecting tax, the postmaster-general could be enjoined from selecting certain roads for the mail route, the secretary or state could be restrained from making treaties. In fact there was no limit if the doctrine were once accepted. But, the Secretary asserted, the Confederate government would not acquiesce; it must insist upon action in spite of the injunction.[1] There is no record as to whether the Confederate government did override the injunction in this case or not, but we know that it had allowed the state courts and the Governor to delay work two years or more, which after all is the point of most importance.

There is one group whom we have thus far alluded to as being opposed to the impressment of property—the state-rights faction in Congress. This group constantly agitated against the system in and out of Congress, and welcomed the obstruction put in the way of the impressment laws by the governors and other state officials. It will not add further interest and knowledge to this subject to follow out the details of this phase of the controversy. Suffice it to say, that, after obstructing and harassing the administration and further adding to the discontent of the people, the state-rights party in Congress succeeded in amending the impress-

[1] O. R., Ser. 4, Vol. III, pp. 660–62.

ment laws in the spring of 1864 so as to be more in accord with their ideas,[1] and in the winter of 1864–65 they finally passed a law that repudiated the entire system of impressment and provided for paying the market price.[2]

By way of summary we may say that impressment was absolutely necessary in 1863; that it was, even when carried out legally, very harsh and unequal in its operation, and that when it was not done according to law it was unbearable; that the Confederate government conceded the evils of the system but contended correctly that it was an "inexorable necessity." The state-rights group denied the necessity and offered bitter opposition to the impressment of supplies, negroes, and railroad iron. They exaggerated the evils greatly, and roused much discontent among the people, causing every imaginable obstruction to be placed in the way of the execution of the law—in short, they finally contributed largely to the breakdown of the system.

[1] *Ibid.*, p. 1151.

[2] *Ibid.*, Ser. 1, Vol. XL, Part II, pp. 1214–16. For the details of the controversy in Congress, see the following: *Journal of the Confederate Congress*, VI, 519, 527, 534, 542, 552–54, 563, 646, 665, 675–77, 692, 786, 829, 830, 835, 863. Also *Annual Cyclopaedia* (1863), pp. 229–30.

CONCLUSION

The idea of state rights and local patriotism resulted in each of the Confederate states undertaking its own local defense, aside from the general defense of the Confederacy. In 1861 this resulted in a shortage of arms and munitions for the general service. The Confederate government had at the outset about 190,000 small arms and about 8,000 cannon, while the states had about 350,000 small arms in addition to the large stock in private hands. In their desire to protect themselves, the states failed to pool all these arms for the general service but kept many of them in their arsenals or placed them in the hands of the local state troops. The result was that about 200,000 volunteers for Confederate service were rejected the first year of the war because the government could not arm them. The reports of Secretaries of War Walker and Benjamin substantiate these figures. This means that if the states had surrendered their arms freely the Confederacy would, with the aid of

imported and captured munitions, have put
600,000 instead of 400,000 men in the field the
first year.

After 1861 it became more a question of men
than arms. Arms a plenty were available to
equip 600,000 men. But by this time the states
had placed in local organizations most of the
surplus man-power willing to fight. It is probable that over 100,000 men were thus held in state
service in the spring of 1862. These troops were
very poor as a rule, not being subject to discipline of a very rigorous kind. We might say that
these 100,000 men were virtually lost to military
service, judged in the light of what they actually
contributed toward the war.

Conscription in 1862 disbanded many of
these. Many were, however, retained, especially
by South Carolina and North Carolina, on the
grounds that they were "troops of war" and not
militia. Soon after this, in spite of the law of
conscription, the states which had lost their
troops began to rebuild the old organizations.
They did so usually with the consent of the Confederate government; but this consent was given
reluctantly and under political duress. Con-

script material composed nine-tenths of these forces. Finally it was determined by the Confederate government to gain control of the state organizations—those above forty-five and between sixteen and seventeen—for local defense under Confederate authority, while those between eighteen and forty-five should be transferred for general service. The conscript law of 1864 attempted this. It failed. The governors, most of them, kept their troops, under the right of keeping "troops of war." Some gave them up, but only when the war had about come to an end.

Thus we see that from a military point of view this local-defense policy did incalculable damage. But this was not all: the attempt of the Confederacy to obtain control of these troops resulted in many bitter quarrels between the Confederate and state authorities, which helped greatly to destroy that spirit of co-operation so essential to a government like the Confederacy.

Not only did the states maintain their own military establishments, but they exercised a considerable control over their troops in Confederate service. Brown and Vance, especially, considered that all Confederate troops were, in reality, militia, and that they had the constitutional right to appoint officers to fill vacancies among these troops.

The states during the first year of the war objected to direct volunteering. They demanded that the troops be raised through, and submitted by, state agency to the Confederate government.

Most important of all was the attempt of each state to supply its troops in Confederate service. By the end of the war the states were controlling 60 out of 122 cotton factories for this purpose, leaving only 62 for Confederate use. North Carolina had 40 cotton mills and did not allow the Confederate government a yard of cloth from them for any except North Carolina troops during the entire war.

The foreign source of supply also experienced this same competition between the states and the Confederacy. Each state did a blockade business wherever possible and, to that extent, withdrew supplies from general distribution, because only a limited amount could run the blockade, and the more the states got the less the Confederacy got. Davis tried to stop this attempt of the states to supply their troops in the Confederate service. He and Secretary of War Seddon both pointed out time after time that this decentralizing policy would result in troops from states like North Carolina, with large domestic equipment and blockade-running facilities, being oversupplied, while troops from interior states or states without manufacturing establishments would be poorly supplied; and that this would create jealousy and discontent in the army and friction between Confederate and state agents. The protests were of no avail. The state-rights party insisted on this individualistic policy in the face of all attempts of the Confederacy to circumvent it. The usual controversy also accompanied the attempts of the Confederacy to assert itself in this business. The results of this policy may be seen in the case of North Carolina. Governor Vance boasted that at the end of the war he had every one of his soldiers well clothed and had on hand in warehouses 92,000 uniforms, thousands of blankets, shoes, and tents. But at the same time Lee's men in Virginia were barefooted, almost without blankets, tents, and clothing. Vance had enough uniforms to give every man in Lee's army two apiece.

The Confederacy, being the invaded country, witnessed a marked decline and frequently a complete collapse of civil government. The only remedy that would restore order and protect the country from spies and disaffection and bush-whacking was the suspension of the writ of habeas corpus, or even martial law. Lincoln, under much milder conditions, suspended the writ and established martial law without congressional sanction. In fact the writ was suspended in the North throughout almost the entire war, either by executive or legislative action. In the South, on the other hand, it was not until 1862, when Donelson and Henry fell and the Confederate armies were forced back to Shiloh, and various points in Virginia and North Carolina were captured, that Congress granted the right to the President to suspend the writ. Even then Davis made use of this law in very few places. This was due to the opposition from the state governments more than anything else. The opposition headed by Stephens, Toombs, Yancey, Brown, and Vance gained such head that Davis was unable to obtain a law to suspend the writ during the whole year of 1863. He was, however, able to get an act passed, February, 1864, suspending the writ in certain cases. But this law raised almost a revolution from the state-rights group, and it was not renewed at its expiration.

The writ was thus allowed to be suspended about one year and four months during the four years of war, and even then Davis had not dared to make a wide use of his right under the laws.

The effect of this was disastrous. Deserters and draft-dodgers, with the aid of judges like Pearson, of North Carolina, Hill and Gray, of Texas, Halyburton and Fuller, of Virginia, obtained writs of habeas corpus and escaped service. Spies and bridge-burners and disloyal peace societies were allowed unrestrained freedom in the absence of either military or civil authority in large parts of the country.

Perhaps as injurious as the conditions rising from the absence of martial law in a country where there was no civil law was the disaffection of the population caused by the opposition of Stephens, Brown, Vance, and other state-rights leaders to the policy of suspending the writ. The people were led to believe that Davis and his government were bent on military despotism, and consequently withheld much of their support.

Conscription was adopted in the spring of 1862. Its chief service was that it stimulated volunteering among men who did not want to be drafted and that it retained the men already in the army whose terms would soon expire, and thus prevented the threatened disintegration of the Confederate army.

The policy of conscription would have resulted in getting many more able-bodied but reluctant gentlemen into the army if it had not been opposed so bitterly by the state-rights leaders. Governor Brown's opposition dated from the first law. He was supported by Vice-Presidents Stephens and Toombs. The argument was that it was unnecessary and unconstitutional; that conscription would destroy the state governments by taking the officers; that it would destroy the state militia, and thus impair state sovereignty. Vance soon became unfriendly and opposed the policy of conscription. In February, 1864, the conscript law, which brought all

279

in from seventeen to eighteen and forty-five to fifty, raised a universal protest. Practically every state entered the list. The governors forced the Confederacy to exempt every state and militia officer from deputy constable to supreme-court judge, as well as state troops to which I have already referred. Even employees in Vance's cotton mills were declared by the state supreme court to be state officers. As a result of this opposition by the states to conscription, 15,000 to 20,000 in North Carolina, 8,000 in Georgia, about half as many in Mississippi and Virginia, about 5,000 in Texas, 2,000 or more in Alabama and South Carolina escaped Confederate military service during the latter part of the war.

The Confederate government was forced to resort to impressment of supplies early in the war because the producers were all holding their goods for higher prices or because they had lost confidence in the Confederate currency. Again, the Confederacy, even where it could obtain the goods by purchase, was unable to pay the market prices without bankruptcy, so it was influenced greatly by the necessity of fixing a low price which it would pay for supplies. At first there was no law covering the practice, but in 1863 impressments were so necessary that a law was passed to regulate the practice. Both negroes and supplies were to be impressed according to its terms. A great wave of indignation swept over the state-rights group. Vance and Brown, aided by Stephens and Toombs, fought the policy from start to finish. South Carolina under Governors Bonham and Magrath entered the list. Watts, of Alabama, joined the ranks—in fact the machinery of most of the states was used to obstruct the law. The controversy further added to the disaffection of the people and destroyed further the spirit of co-operation. Finally, impressment broke down and the Confederacy was forced to buy in the open market.

INDEX

INDEX

INDEX

Rector, *see* Arkansas

Richmond: armory at, 14; under martial law, 152

Roberts, S. A., 83

Robertson, J., 251

Ruggles, General, 37

Savannah, Confederate cargo at, 19

Seacoast, 128, 151

Seddon, Secretary of War, 237; on impressment, 264; letters, 33; refutes accusations, 70

Sherman, W. T., 63

Shipping, 131

Shorter, *see* Alabama

Simms, William, 221

Skeleton regiments, 86, 87

Smith, General, in Texas, 60

South Carolina: arms, 9; Board of Relief of Soldiers' Families, 213; Eighteenth Regiment, 41; Governor Bonham, 132; impressment of slaves in, 257; impressment in, 249; legislature, on Confederate contracts, 132, on conscription, 211; local defense troops, 26, 41, 44; nullification sentiment in, 257; state troops, 13

South Carolina College, 213

Sovereignty of states, 3, 6, 52, 142, 145; *see* state rights

Speculation, 219

State rights, 2, 6, 79, 272; and conscription, 51; faction in Congress, 191, 270; leaders, 4; reaction, 213; usurpation of, 108

Stephens, Alexander Hamilton, 2, 162, 184, 185, 187

Stephens, Linton, 185

Stephens-Toombs-Brown-Vance party, 53

Stovall's battalion, 29

Surface, John, 194

Supplies, 219; of arms in states, 8; common purchase of, 112; distribution of, 110; foreign, 275; purchased abroad, 128; results of individualism, 111; state provision, 110; surplus of, 126; in Virginia, 117

Supply department, 112

Taylor, W. H., General, 195

Tennessee, 5; Governor Harris, 26; state troops, 14

Texas, 5; arms, 9; conscription in, 62; defense in, 82; extreme state rights, 61; Governor Lubbock, 82; Governor Murrah, 60; legislature, 60, on direct enlistment, 82; local defense, 27; under martial law, 157; state troops, 14, 41, 59

Toombs, Robert, 2, 88, 162, 233

Trading with the enemy, 201

Trenholme, Secretary of the Treasury, 201, 236

Troops, state, in Confederate service, 76

Twelve-months men, 99, 100, 103

Vance, Zebulon, 2, 38, 43, 173; quarrel with Davis, 39, 97; *see* North Carolina

289

PRINTED IN THE U.S.A.